REMIND THEM

of His

COVENANT FAITHFULNESS

APMI Publications
a division of Kingdom Dimension Books
P.O. Box 17,
55051 Barga (LU),
Tuscany, Italy

REMIND THEM
of His

COVENANT FAITHFULNESS

ISRAEL
THE CHURCH AND THE KINGDOM OF GOD

DRS. ALAN AND JENNIFER
PATEMAN

BOOK TITLE:
Remind them of His Covenant Faithfulness
–Israel, the Church and the Kingdom of God

This edition published in 2025

Published by APMI Publications
A Division of Kingdom Dimension Books, Library No. **84**
P.O. Box 17,
55051 Barga (LU),
Italy

Email: publications@alanpatemanworldmissions.com
www.AlanPatemanWorldMissions.com

**APMI Publications and Kingdom Dimension Books are a division of
Alan Pateman World Missions**

Printed in the United States of America, Europe and Asia

Paperback ISBN: 978-1-918102-07-9
eBook ISBN: 978-1-918102-08-6

Acknowledgements:
Author/Design/Senior Editor/Publisher: Apostle Dr. Alan Pateman
Co-Author/Editing/Proofreading/Research: Pastor Dr. Jennifer Pateman
Computer Administration/Office Manager: Dr. Dorothea Struhlik
Cover Image Credit: www.PosterMyWall.com

*Where scriptures appear with special emphasis (**in bold,** italic or underlined) we have edited them ourselves in order to bring focused attention within the context of this subject being taught.*

Any theology that teaches
that God has cast away His ancient people
will soon teach that
He can cast away His new people also.
But His covenant stands fast forever.

— Charles H. Spurgeon

I will bless those who bless you,
and curse him who curses you;
and in you all families of the earth
shall be blessed.

– Gen 12:3

God's promises are not revoked. His purposes are not replaced. The Church is grafted in by grace – not in place. From covenant to kingdom, His story continues still.

This book exists to confront the lie and proclaim the truth: **ISRAEL IS NOT DONE:** *"Though I make a full end of all nations where I have scattered you, yet <u>I will not make a full end of you</u>" (Jer 30:11).*

❖

Dedication

To the Peace of Jerusalem

Pray for the peace of Jerusalem:
They shall prosper that love thee.

— Ps 122 KJV

❖

Table of Contents

Preface...13

Acknowledgement..15

Introduction...17

Chapter 1   The God Who Calls..............................21

Chapter 2   Israel: Chosen for a Purpose...............25

Chapter 3   The Faithfulness of God in Israel's History....29

Chapter 4   Jesus: The Fulfilment, not the Cancellation....33

Chapter 5   Pentecost: The Renewal of Israel.........39

Chapter 6   The Gentile Mission:
             Grafted in not Replaced........................45

Chapter 7   Physical & Spiritual Israel:
             Distinct but not Mutually Exclusive.......53

Chapter 8   The Olive Tree of Covenant Mercy.......59

Chapter 9   The Israel of God................................65

Chapter 10   Israel's King & The Kingdom of God.............73

Chapter 11   The Universal Lordship of Our Messiah.........81

Chapter 12   The New Jerusalem..............................87

Chapter 13   The Church's Obligation to Israel..............95

Chapter 14   The Error of Replacement Theology............101

Chapter 15   The Peace of Jerusalem.......................109

Chapter 16   Final Words on:
                  The Delegitimisation of Israel................119

    Epilogue....................................125

    Note on Referenced Authors...................129

    Quotes: From Notable Public Figures..........131

    Endnotes....................................143

❖

Preface

My wife and I have written this book together because we were experiencing a growing burden that weighed heavily on both our hearts. And for the record, we never set out to write *just another book* — far from it. It was as we watched this old error resurfacing in sermons, conversations, and Christian media *(socials, podcasts etc)*, that we felt a deep concern rising. It grieved the Holy Spirit within us. In fact the more we prayed, the more restless we became, until we had to put our thoughts down on paper. His whisper became unmistakable: *"Remind them."*

Of what? His faithfulness — that **He is the covenant-making, and covenant-keeping God.** His word has not changed, and all of His covenants still stand. He is the Rock of Ages *(Isa 26:4)* — not a pebble, not shifting sand. Our foundation is built upon that Rock. If one covenant can be questioned, then all are called into doubt—and with them, the very security of our salvation.

It's a subtle and dangerous deception: convince people that sin is merely a condition to be managed, and they stop seeking a Saviour. Remove sin, and there is no need for redemption. Remove the covenants, and there are no promises left to keep. But God is faithful. His covenants are the anchors of His character, and His promises are the pillars of our hope.

This is why these pages exist: not to argue theology, but to rekindle love—love for Israel, love for the Church *(the body of Christ),* and love for the God who never forgets His promises. We write because we believe we are living in a time when truth must be spoken again, clearly and with compassion.

Our prayer is that as you read, something awakens in your spirit—a remembrance of the faithfulness of God, a reverence for His plan, and a renewed gratitude that what He began in Israel, He is completing in Christ for the sake of all nations.

May this book be a call to return—to truth, to covenant, and to the God who still says of Israel, *"You are Mine."*

❖

Acknowledgement

This work draws on the heritage of both synagogue and church, on the scriptures preserved by Israel and the gospel proclaimed by her Messiah. Gratitude is due to countless scholars, teachers, and faithful communities who have laboured to understand the unity of God's purpose through history.

Special appreciation belongs to those who read these pages not as a debate to win, but as a journey to undertake — seeking to rediscover the wonder of a God who is faithful to His word. Though these pages contend for truth, may every discussion they inspire be marked by humility, reverence, and hope.

And above all, thanks be to our **COVENANT MAKING & KEEPING GOD.** The God of Abraham, Isaac, and Jacob, and whose covenant love endures forever.

❖

Introduction

Here We Go Again: Trapped in the "Replacement Theology" Echo Chamber
(When the Church forgets Her Roots)

There's a growing concern about the rise of the reoccurring error of *replacement theology* — the idea that the Church has replaced Israel in God's plan. This has been our main burden in prayer and the reason for revisiting this subject. Many of the teachers who once stood firm on biblical truth regarding Israel — voices of the old bible scholars such as Derek Prince — are slowly fading away, while a new generation of voices is emerging.

There's a stirring in the Spirit to speak once more about this teaching that refuses to stay buried — an old error wearing a new face, rising again in a generation that doesn't remember the battles already fought and won. *Replacement theology* is a persistent false teaching that has resurfaced time and again throughout church history — and now, more than ever, the Church must once again "clean house."

Many new voices are embracing old errors as if they were new. It's like those who discover Marxism for the first time — they don't understand the cost. Unlike second-generation Cubans, for example, who still live with its effects. This misunderstanding severs the Church from her roots and blinds her to the enduring faithfulness of God toward His people, Israel.

Even within the wider world of Christian media and online influence, this trend is spreading. There are organised efforts to shape the narrative about Israel, and social media platforms are playing a significant role. Some political and religious leaders have even discussed the importance of mobilising younger voices online so that the biblical story of Israel is not lost. The concern is that mainstream evangelical circles — especially in the West — are increasingly embracing ideas rooted in *replacement theology* simply out of ignorance.

It's like people swallowing chalk, thinking they're taking vitamins — they read what's on the label but never understand the true ingredients. That's the danger of unexamined teaching.

The Church must once again confront these distortions. The truth remains that the story of redemption is deeply tied to Israel. Pentecost itself was the fulfilment of prophecy to the Jewish people — about a divided Israel being restored and the promise being opened to the nations. The prophetic narrative is centred on Israel, whether people are comfortable with that or not.

The truth remains unchanging: God's covenant with Israel is everlasting. Pentecost was not a new beginning disconnected from the past — it was the fulfilment of ancient promises to the Jewish people, the first sign of Israel's restoration, and the opening of salvation to the nations. From Abraham's call to the outpouring of the Spirit, the thread of God's purpose has never been broken.

When the Church forgets this, she loses sight of her foundation. The gospel does not replace Israel; it fulfils God's promises through her. Grace does not cancel covenant; it confirms it. The story of redemption begins in Jerusalem and flows outward to the ends of the earth — and in the end, it returns there again.

❖

CHAPTER 1

The God Who Calls

THE PATTERN OF DIVINE INITIATIVE

God's call originates from His own initiative. Every movement in the biblical story begins with divine initiative. The God of the Hebrew scriptures is not distant or reactive; He speaks first, calls first, and commits Himself by promise. In Genesis 12 the call to Abram sets a new course for humanity. God's summons — "Go from your country… to the land that I will show you" — creates both a people and a purpose. From that moment the bible traces a single thread: a God who binds Himself to His word.

COVENANT AS THE FRAMEWORK OF SCRIPTURE

Covenant provides the structural backbone of the biblical narrative. The call to Abraham is formalised in covenant.

Unlike human contracts, a covenant in the ancient Near East bound the stronger party to protect the weaker. In Genesis 15 God passes between the pieces of the sacrifice alone, signalling that the fulfilment of the promise rests on Him. Later texts — Exodus 19, Deuteronomy 7, 2 Samuel 7 — repeat this pattern. Each covenant amplifies the previous one rather than erasing it. Across centuries the prophets appeal to that faithfulness: the God who called Abraham continues to call Israel.

A PEOPLE CHOSEN FOR VOCATION, NOT PRIVILEGE

Election implies vocation: chosen for service, not superiority. The choice of Abraham's family is never portrayed as favouritism. Israel's election is a calling to service — "in you all families of the earth shall be blessed." The same God who calls also sends. Through the covenant, Israel is invited to model justice, mercy, and loyalty to one God amid polytheistic cultures. The call therefore carries ethical weight: divine relationship always issues in responsibility.

CONTINUITY AND PROMISE

The consistency of God's call grounds the entire theology of hope. Later writers pick up this theme of unbroken purpose. The psalmists recount the call as the reason for hope *("He remembers His covenant forever," Ps 105:8)*. The prophets argue that despite exile or failure, God's call cannot be annulled. When Paul later writes that "the gifts and the calling of God are irrevocable" *(Rom 11:29)*, he is echoing this long tradition of covenant fidelity.

THE HUMAN RESPONSE

Faithful response completes the covenant relationship. Every covenant also demands response—trust and obedience. Abraham's act of leaving his homeland becomes the archetype of faith. The same dynamic reappears in the lives of Moses, David, and the prophetic community. To be called is to be summoned into a story larger than oneself, one that depends on divine reliability rather than human perfection.

THEOLOGICAL REFLECTION

God's call is the first movement in the story of redemption. Every covenant begins not with human ambition but with divine initiative. *"We love Him, because He first loved us"* *(1 John 4:19 KJV).* His love always makes the first move; our obedience is never the origin but the response. The same God who called Abram still speaks, summoning faith and surrender through His unchanging word. His call creates both identity and destiny—a people shaped by His promise and sustained by His presence. Covenant, therefore, is not a human bargain *(negotiation)* but a divine commitment, written in mercy and upheld by faithfulness.

THEOLOGICAL IMPLICATION

Divine initiative secures the stability of every covenant. What God begins, He Himself sustains. Israel's story—and by extension the Church's mission—rests not upon human resolve but upon God's reliability. The call of God is both invitation and assurance: the One who summons is the One who completes.

The impulse to pursue God originates with God, but the outworking of that impulse is our following hard after Him.

— A. W. Tozer[1]

Redemption begins with God. It is God who takes the initiative; our part is to respond in faith to what He has already done.

— Derek Prince[2]

When He calls, He also endows with power. The call of God is no mere invitation; it has in it a secret drawing power which subdues the will and secures obedience.

— Charles H. Spurgeon[3]

Thus, redemption begins where love began — with God's initiative, to which faith becomes the eternal reply.

❖

CHAPTER 2

Israel: Chosen for a Purpose

ELECTION IN THE STORY OF SCRIPTURE

Election is rooted in divine love, not merit. From the moment God calls Abram, the concept of election enters biblical thought. Israel's existence is the result of divine choice, not human achievement. The early texts stress that this choice rests solely on God's love and promise:

> It was not because you were more numerous than other peoples that the Lord set his heart on you and chose you... but because the Lord loved you and kept the oath he swore to your ancestors.
>
> Deut. 7:7-8

Election, therefore, is relational rather than competitive. Israel's calling is not to boast of privilege but to demonstrate covenant loyalty so that the nations may recognise the God who saves.

A PRIESTLY NATION

Israel's role is priestly—mediating knowledge of God to the world. At Sinai the purpose of election is spelled out in vocational language: "You shall be to me a Kingdom of priests and a holy nation" (Exod 19:6).

To be "priestly" means to stand between God and the world—to embody holiness, justice, and mercy so that creation can be reconciled to its Creator. The Torah gives Israel the structures—ritual, ethical law, and communal rhythm—through which this priestly witness is enacted.

PROPHETIC EXPANSION OF THE CALL

Prophets interpret election as ethical responsibility. Israel's prophets continually remind the nation of this vocation. Isaiah portrays Israel as a light to the nations (Isa 42:6; 49:6). Amos insists that election carries moral responsibility: "You only have I known of all the families of the earth; therefore I will punish you for all your iniquities" (Amos 3:2).

The prophets hold together two truths—God's enduring love for Israel and His demand that this love be mirrored in justice and compassion.

FAITHFULNESS AND FAILURE

Israel's failures highlight God's unbreakable faithfulness. The biblical narrative does not idealise Israel. The same people called to reveal God's holiness often fall short. Yet each cycle of rebellion and renewal highlights God's steadfast commitment to His covenant. Exile becomes both judgment and invitation: a painful means of returning to the original purpose. Jeremiah and Ezekiel envision restoration not as mere political recovery but as spiritual transformation—a heart of stone replaced with a heart of flesh (Ezek 36:26).

UNIVERSAL HORIZON

The covenant's goal is universal blessing through one chosen nation. Israel's vocation always included the nations. The covenant with Abraham already anticipated a global reach — "in you all families of the earth shall be blessed." The later scriptures imagine that future in concrete terms: pilgrims from many peoples streaming to Zion to learn God's ways (Isa 2:2-3; Mic 4:1-2). The divine election of one people is thus the instrument of blessing for all.

THEOLOGICAL REFLECTION

Divine election is not an end in itself but a summons to service. God's choice of Israel reveals His sovereign love and redemptive intent for all creation. To be chosen is to carry purpose: to reflect God's holiness and to make His salvation known among the nations.

Israel's vocation is priestly, mediating between heaven and earth—a living testimony that divine privilege always entails divine responsibility. Even when Israel falters, the faithfulness of God remains the thread unbroken; His election continues, not because of human merit, but because His word and love are unchangeable.

THEOLOGICAL IMPLICATION

Election reveals the missionary heart of God. Through one chosen people, He unveils His purpose for every people. Israel's story shows that divine favour is never about exclusion but extension—blessing flowing outward through covenant faithfulness until all nations know His name. In chapter 3 of his book called, *"Israel: Chosen for a Purpose"* Derek Prince explains the covenant reason behind Israel's election—that God's call was never about privilege or exclusivity, but about vocation and service to the world:

> *"Israel was not chosen for privilege, but for a purpose – to serve God's plan for all nations. Through them, God intended that salvation should come to the whole world."*
> —Derek Prince[1]

> *"God's choice of a man, or of a people, is not a piece of arbitrary partiality. He elects with a purpose. He blesses them that they may be a blessing. His election is not a stagnant pool, but a flowing stream."*
> —Charles H. Spurgeon[2]

> *"When God calls a man He does not call him for himself alone, but that through him He might reach others. God's blessings are never meant to be selfishly enjoyed. The man who is blessed becomes a channel of blessing to those about him."*
> —A. W. Tozer[3]

Thus, Israel's election stands as both revelation and commission—the pattern of a God who calls, blesses, and sends so that His covenant mercy may reach the ends of the earth.

❖

CHAPTER 3

The Faithfulness of God in Israel's History

COVENANT MEMORY IN THE HEBREW BIBLE

Israel's memory preserves awareness of God's steadfast acts. Israel's identity depends on remembering what God has done. The Psalms and historical writings repeatedly recall the Exodus, Sinai, and the promises to the patriarchs. This memory forms the moral and theological spine of the nation:

> He remembers His covenant forever, the word that He commanded for a thousand generations.
>
> Ps 105:8

In a world of shifting loyalties, divine remembrance becomes the guarantor of stability.

THE PATTERN OF REBELLION AND RENEWAL

Historical cycles of failure highlight divine mercy. The narrative of Judges, Kings, and Chronicles reveals a cyclical rhythm: disobedience, judgment, repentance, and restoration. The cycle underscores that while human faithfulness falters, divine mercy endures. Even when the kingdom collapses, the prophets interpret disaster as correction, not abandonment. The covenant remains the unseen anchor through national failure.

EXILE AS THE CRUCIBLE OF FAITH

Exile refines covenant hope rather than cancels it. The Babylonian exile transforms Israel's understanding of covenant. Without temple, king, or land, faith shifts from ritual to trust in the enduring word of God. Jeremiah's new covenant promise (Jer 31:31–34) and Ezekiel's vision of a restored people (Ezek 36–37) reveal that exile purifies hope rather than extinguishes it. God's presence follows His people into captivity.

RESTORATION AND EXPECTATION

Post-exilic faith lives between partial and final restoration. The return from exile under Cyrus fulfils prophetic promises yet leaves anticipation unfulfilled. Though Jerusalem is rebuilt, the deeper restoration—the renewal of hearts—remains future. Post-exilic writings such as Haggai, Zechariah, and Malachi sustain this tension: God has acted, yet His ultimate purpose awaits completion. Israel learns to live between promise and fulfilment.

THEOLOGICAL IMPLICATIONS OF FAITHFULNESS

God's reliability becomes the theological thread linking both Testaments. The continuity of divine fidelity becomes a cornerstone of biblical theology. Later writers interpret Israel's survival as testimony that God's word cannot fail. This theme carries directly into the New Testament, where Paul cites the same principle: "What if some were unfaithful? Does their faithlessness nullify the faithfulness of God? By no means" (Rom 3:3–4). **Faithfulness defines God's character and underwrites all covenant hope.**

When it comes to God's faithfulness demonstrated in Israel, Derek Prince explains that the enduring covenant relationship between God and Israel is the clearest evidence of His unchanging nature. He draws the direct parallel that the Church's confidence in God's promises rests on this same demonstrated faithfulness:

> *If God has been faithful to Israel for more than four thousand years, through all their disobedience and rebellion, He will be faithful to the Church also. God's covenant with Israel is the pattern of His covenant with us.*
>
> — Derek Prince[1]

> *The Lord's faithfulness is the shield and stay of His people. He has not cast away Israel, nor will He ever cast away any whom He has chosen.*
>
> — Charles H. Spurgeon[2]

> *God's faithfulness is the foundation of His covenant engagements. Were He unfaithful for a moment, the whole framework of redemption would collapse.*
>
> — A. W. Pink[3]

Thus, Israel's endurance becomes living proof that covenant faithfulness is not merely a doctrine to affirm but a testimony that unfolds through time—God's unbroken word written across history.

❖

CHAPTER 4

Jesus: The Fulfilment, Not the Cancellation

THE CONTINUITY OF THE STORY

J esus stands within, not outside, Israel's covenant line. The New Testament begins not with a new idea but with a genealogy (Matt 1:1–17). Its opening words — "The book of the genealogy of Jesus Christ, the son of David, the son of Abraham" — anchor Jesus within Israel's covenant line. He is introduced as the heir of the promises made to the patriarchs and the royal descendant through whom those promises reach completion. The continuity between the Testaments is deliberate: the same God who called Abraham now acts through Abraham's seed

JESUS, THE LAW & THE PROPHETS

His mission fulfils the Law and the Prophets rather than abolishing them. In the Sermon on the Mount Jesus addresses the question of discontinuity directly: "Do not think that I have come to abolish the Law or the Prophets; I have not come to abolish them but to fulfil them" (Matt 5:17).

Fulfilment *(plērōsai)* means to bring something to its intended goal. Jesus' teaching, life, and death reveal the meaning latent *(hidden)* in the Torah rather than rendering it obsolete. He interprets the Sabbath, purity, and sacrifice in ways that uncover their ethical and redemptive core — mercy, wholeness, and reconciliation.

THE COVENANT IN HIS OWN BLOOD

The New Covenant in His blood realises Jeremiah's vision of internal transformation. At the Last Supper Jesus reinterprets the Passover meal in covenantal language: "This cup is the New Covenant in my blood" (Luke 22:20; cf. Jer 31:31-34).

The setting is crucial: a Jewish festival commemorating deliverance from Egypt. By framing His impending death within that liturgy, Jesus presents Himself as the decisive act of divine faithfulness. The New Covenant does not erase the Old; it realises its deepest intention — law written on the heart, forgiveness secured, relationship restored.

THE MESSIAH OF ISRAEL AND SAVIOUR OF THE WORLD

As Israel's Messiah, Jesus extends covenant blessing to all nations. The Gospels portray Jesus as the long-awaited Messiah who extends Israel's calling to the nations. His mission follows the pattern "to the Jew first and also to the Greek" (Matt 10:5-6; Rom 1:16). The earliest community around Him remained Jewish, yet His message contained a universal horizon. In Him the Abrahamic promise — "in you all families of the earth shall be blessed" — moves from prophecy to reality.

THE CROSS AS COVENANT FULFILMENT

On the cross, the themes of sacrifice, priesthood, and kingship converge. The Passover Lamb, the Suffering Servant, and the Righteous King find unity in one event. Early Christian writers interpreted the resurrection as God's vindication of His covenant faithfulness: the same power that brought Israel from Egypt now raises the Messiah from death. Through Him, covenant faith extends beyond ethnicity to encompass all who trust in God's promise.

FULFILMENT VERSUS REPLACEMENT

Fulfilment means completion of promise, not replacement of people: This distinction between fulfilment and replacement is central. The New Covenant represents continuity in purpose with transformation in scope. The God who was faithful to Israel remains faithful through Christ, whose life embodies the obedience Israel was called to display. **The promise is expanded, not revoked; the covenantal root still nourishes the new growth.**

THEOLOGICAL REFLECTION

In Jesus, the covenant story reaches its goal, not its grave. The Word made flesh steps into Israel's history — not to cancel it, but to complete it. The same God who called Abraham and spoke through Moses now speaks through His Son, the heir of every promise. The cross is not the end of covenant but its confirmation—the Passover renewed, the temple fulfilled, the law written on hearts. In Christ, mercy triumphs over failure, and faithfulness extends from Israel to every nation. The root remains; the branches are renewed. In Him, every promise of God finds its "Yes and Amen."

THEOLOGICAL IMPLICATION

To see Christ rightly is to see continuity, not contrast. The faithfulness of God in Israel becomes visible in the face of Jesus. Every covenant finds its telos in Him—the faithful Israelite who embodies obedience, mercy, and truth. The New Covenant is not another story but the same story brought to completion. Therefore, those who follow Christ share in Israel's calling: to live as witnesses of divine faithfulness so that the nations may know the God who keeps His word.

> *The covenant was not destroyed in Christ, but fulfilled; the sacrifices and ceremonies of the law were but shadows, and in Him they find their substance. What was symbol is now reality, what was promise is now fulfilment.*
>
> —A. B. Simpson[1]

> *"The Cross is the highest expression of God's love; it meets the demands of His righteousness, satisfies the claims of His holiness, and fulfils the requirements of His justice."* He then quotes Psalm 85:10: *"It is there that mercy and truth meet together, righteousness and peace kiss each other."*
>
> —Watchman Nee[2]

The New Covenant did not cancel the old; it revealed its true meaning. God's plan did not change with Israel's failure, because His purpose was eternal, completed in Christ Jesus.

— Benny Hinn[3]

Thus, Jesus stands as the living intersection of every divine promise — the faithfulness of God embodied, the covenant complete, and the blessing of Abraham extended to the ends of the earth.

❖

CHAPTER 5

Pentecost: The Renewal of Israel

FROM PROMISE TO FULFILMENT

Pentecost fulfils prophetic promises of Israel's renewal. Before His ascension, Jesus told the disciples to remain in Jerusalem until they received "the promise of the Father" (Acts 1:4-5). That promise echoed Joel 2:28-32 and other prophetic visions of Israel's spiritual renewal. Pentecost—the Jewish feast of Shavuot, fifty days after Passover—became the appointed time when those hopes burst into reality. What occurs in Acts 2 is not the birth of a new religion but the renewal of the covenant people by the Spirit of God.

A JEWISH GATHERING

The event occurs entirely within a Jewish context. The setting underlines continuity with Israel's story. The upper-room community consisted of the eleven apostles, now restored to twelve with Matthias, together with Mary and other Jewish believers. The pilgrims who heard the sound of the rushing wind were "devout Jews from every nation under heaven" (Acts 2:5) — Diaspora Jews and proselytes gathered for the festival. The event therefore begins within Israel's historical and religious life, fulfilling the ancient expectation that God would pour out His Spirit upon His people.

THE SPIRIT AS THE SIGN OF COVENANT RENEWAL

The Spirit's descent internalises covenant holiness. In the prophets, the gift of the Spirit marked the moment when God would cleanse His people and write His law upon their hearts (Ezek 36:26-27; Jer 31:33). The tongues of fire in Acts 2 recall Sinai's flame, now resting not on a mountain but on individuals. The same divine presence that once dwelt in the tabernacle now fills the community. The covenant is internalised; holiness becomes a matter of transformed life rather than ritual boundary.

PETER'S INTERPRETATION

Peter interprets the event as fulfilment, not innovation and his sermon anchors the phenomenon in scripture. Citing Joel, he explains that what is happening belongs to "the last days" — the era of fulfilment long anticipated by Israel's prophets. His call to repentance and baptism "in the name of Jesus the Messiah" (Acts 2:38) unites covenant renewal with recognition of the risen Christ. About three thousand respond, forming the nucleus of a renewed Israel defined by faith and Spirit rather than lineage alone.

THE COMMUNITY THAT EMERGES

The first believers embody Israel's priestly vocation. The portrait of the early believers at the end of Acts 2 reflects Israel's ideal vocation: steadfast in teaching, fellowship, shared resources, and prayer. The phrase "they continued daily in the temple" (Acts 2:46) shows that they still viewed themselves within Israel's worshiping life. The Spirit's work creates continuity, not separation — an Israel made new from within.

TOWARD THE NATIONS

The movement outward to the nations extends Israel's mission, preserving continuity with her calling. While Pentecost begins in Jerusalem, it carries centrifugal energy. Jesus had said, "You will be my witnesses in Jerusalem and in all Judea and Samaria and to the ends of the earth" (Acts 1:8). The sequence unfolds through Acts: Jewish believers first, Samaritans next, and finally Gentiles such as Cornelius. The mission to the nations is therefore an extension of Israel's renewal, not its replacement.

THEOLOGICAL REFLECTION

Pentecost affirms the continuity of God's covenant faithfulness through a new and living phase. What began at Sinai with law written on stone finds its fulfilment at Zion with law inscribed upon hearts. The same God who descended in fire now indwells His people by the Spirit; the same covenant that once thundered from a mountain now speaks within the soul, saying, *"I will dwell in them, and walk in them"* (2 Cor 6:16 KJV).

The fire that once crowned a mountain now rests upon a people. The mission that began with Israel's call to bless the nations now receives power for its worldwide reach. Pentecost, therefore, is not replacement but renewal—the divine presence moving from temple to hearts, from nation to nations.

THEOLOGICAL IMPLICATION

The descent of the Spirit confirms that God's covenant fidelity has not failed but advanced. Through the Spirit, Israel's vocation—to bless all nations—receives power for its global commission. Pentecost reveals a God who fulfils, not forsakes; who renews His people so that His purpose may reach the ends of the earth. The same faithfulness that gathered Israel now gathers the nations into one redemptive story.

> *The Holy Spirit did not come to replace Israel, but to continue what God began through Israel and to send the fire of the Gospel to the ends of the earth.*
>
> —Reinhard Bonnke[1]

> *The indwelling of the Spirit is the bond of union between the Father and His children; He is Himself the seal and the power of the covenant within.*
>
> —Andrew Murray[2]

Pentecost came after prayer. The fire fell where the sacrifice was ready; prayer had prepared the altar, and obedience kept it burning.

— E. M. Bounds[3]

Thus, Pentecost reveals the faithfulness of the covenant God who renews His people by His Spirit, ensuring that the flame kindled in Israel continues to light the nations.

❖

CHAPTER 6

The Gentile Mission: Grafted in not Replaced

THE EXPANSION FORETOLD

This chapter traces how the gospel's expansion to the nations follows, rather than cancels, Israel's covenant purpose. The Gentile mission fulfils prophetic expectation.

Long before the events of Acts, the Hebrew prophets envisioned a day when the nations would join in worship of Israel's God. "Many peoples shall come and say: 'Come, let us go up to the mountain of the Lord... for out of Zion shall go forth the law'" (Isa 2:3).

The covenant with Abraham carried this same horizon: "In you all the families of the earth shall be blessed." The

Gentile mission therefore stands as the extension, not the alteration, of Israel's original vocation.

FROM JERUSALEM TO THE NATIONS

The book of Acts portrays expansion from Jerusalem to the ends of the earth; traces a deliberate geographical and theological sequence:

- **Jerusalem** — the Spirit poured out on Israel (Acts 2).

- **Judea and Samaria** — the gospel crosses internal boundaries (Acts 8).

- **The ends of the earth** — Gentiles receive the same Spirit (Acts 10).

The command of Acts 1:8 becomes the structural outline of the entire narrative, showing that the global reach of the gospel is the logical outcome of God's promises to Israel.

CORNELIUS AND THE SECOND PENTECOST

Cornelius' conversion mirrors Pentecost and confirms divine initiative. The turning point arrives with the Roman centurion Cornelius. His story parallels Pentecost: angelic vision, apostolic preaching, and the outpouring of the Spirit. Peter recognises the significance immediately:

The Holy Spirit fell on them just as on us at the beginning.

Acts 11:15

The inclusion of Gentiles occurs by divine initiative; no human council decrees it. God Himself grants them the same gift given to Israel, proving that the covenant blessing has opened to all who believe.

THE JERUSALEM COUNCIL: UNITY WITHOUT UNIFORMITY

The Jerusalem Council affirms inclusion without assimilation. In Acts 15, the apostles confront the practical implications of Gentile inclusion. Must Gentiles adopt Jewish law to belong? Citing Amos 9:11-12 – "I will rebuild the fallen tent of David... that the rest of mankind may seek the Lord" – James concludes that Gentile believers are welcomed as Gentiles. The decision preserves unity without erasing distinction: the nations enter the covenant community through faith in Israel's Messiah, not through ethnic conversion.

PAUL'S THEOLOGY OF THE OLIVE TREE

Paul's olive tree image unites Jew and Gentile in one covenant root. Romans 11 provides the fullest theological reflection on this process. Paul describes Israel's covenant as a cultivated olive tree. Some branches *(unbelieving Jews)* are broken off, and wild shoots *(believing Gentiles)* are grafted in. Yet the root – the patriarchal covenant – remains the same. Paul warns Gentile believers:

> Do not be arrogant toward the branches... remember it is not you who support the root, but the root that supports you.
>
> Rom 11:18

The metaphor rules out both Jewish exclusivism and Gentile triumphalism. The tree remains one, sustained by God's enduring promises.

THE GOAL: MUTUAL FULFILMENT

God's plan aims at the ultimate reconciliation of both Israel and the nations. Paul foresees a future reconciliation when Israel's partial hardening will end and "all Israel will be saved" (Rom 11:26). The fullness of the Gentiles and the restoration of Israel belong to the same divine plan. God's mercy weaves both stories into one. The inclusion of Gentiles is not an alternative to Israel's redemption but the means through which it comes to completion.

THE CHARACTER OF THE MISSION

The Church's posture must remain humble, grateful, and mission-oriented. Because the Gentile mission reveals the heart of God's faithfulness. It demonstrates that election is missional: chosen people become channels of blessing. The Church's task is to embody humility toward its Jewish root and generosity toward all nations. The grafting image defines the relationship: **dependence on the same covenantal root, shared participation in its fruit.**

THEOLOGICAL REFLECTION

The Gentile mission reveals not a new tree but new branches grafted into an ancient root. From Abraham's call to Paul's commission, God's purpose has always moved outward through Israel's covenant. The same grace that chose a nation now embraces the nations, binding Jew and Gentile into one redeemed family. The gospel's reach does not erase Israel's identity; it magnifies her calling as the vessel of blessing. What began in Jerusalem continues across the earth — one covenant, one Messiah, one Spirit breathing life into every branch.

THEOLOGICAL IMPLICATION

The grafting of the nations into Israel's covenant demands humility and gratitude. Gentile believers stand by faith, sustained by promises they did not originate. The root supports the branches; the covenant sustains the mission. God's plan is reconciliation, not replacement — mutual fulfilment that glorifies the faithfulness of the One who unites all peoples in His mercy.

In one of Spurgeon's clearest affirmations of God's continuing covenant faithfulness to Israel — he said the following:

> *The grafting in of the wild olive was wonderful grace indeed; but what shall we say of the natural branches when they shall be grafted in again? It will be glory upon glory, the triumph of mercy and the fulfilment of the covenant.*
> — Charles H. Spurgeon[1]

> *The Church does not take Israel's place; she takes her place with Israel in the purpose of God.*
> — Derek Prince[2]

> *The Church has no life apart from Christ. She exists to express Him. All her activities, her ministry, and her unity come from Him as the source. The branches cannot live of themselves; they draw all their supply from the root.*
> — Watchman Nee[3]

Thus, the Gentile mission is the flowering of Israel's promise — many branches sharing one life, nourished by the same covenant root, until all nations rejoice in the mercy of Israel's God.

AUTHORS' NOTE:
OUR ROOT & PRIMARY ALLEGIANCE IS CHRIST

Before we move on to the next chapter, we want to add a short caveat to address a common and growing concern that Christ is our root — not Israel — and that our first *"allegiance is to Christ, not Israel."* These voices can be overwhelming and convincing, yet we respond not in the spirit of debate — which has sadly become the new sport — but with dignity and with a respect for the older teachers whose voices — though fading — left a rich legacy. **It is that legacy we have sought to uphold in this book, without losing any of the freshness of today's manna — the now word of God — the spoken sayings of God for this generation.**

In every generation, believers have wrestled with how Israel and the Church belong together. Certain teachers — Scofield, Spurgeon, Nee, and others — spoke within frameworks later labelled *dispensational* or *covenantal,* yet their hearts burned with one conviction: **God keeps His word.**

To recognise Israel's enduring covenant is not to diminish Christ, but to magnify His faithfulness through the people He first called. **Christ is the root of salvation, and that root grew in Israel's soil.** The olive tree of Romans 11 is one living story in which Jew and Gentile share the same life.

Rather than arguing over labels, may we recover wonder at the faithfulness of the God who grafts us in by grace — and who continues to speak His living word afresh to every generation. *(Clarifying Note: And by this we do not mean new scripture or additional revelation. The canon of scripture is complete. God still speaks today by His Spirit — never in contradiction to the written word, but always in harmony with it — bringing what is written to life in each generation).*

EXTRA CLARIFYING NOTE CONCERNING THE "NOW WORD OF GOD"

THE LIVING WORD (RHEMA) & THE WRITTEN WORD (LOGOS):

When we speak of the *now word of God* or the *living word,* we are not referring to new scripture, nor adding to what has been written. The canon of scripture is closed — complete, sufficient, and inspired by the Spirit once for all. Yet the same Spirit who breathed the word continues to breathe through it, bringing timeless truth into timely relevance. God still speaks — never in contradiction to scripture, but always in harmony with it — illuminating hearts, guiding His people, and applying His eternal word to present circumstances. His voice today is not *new revelation* but *fresh realisation.*

THE SPIRIT WHO INSPIRED THE WORD STILL ILLUMINATES IT TODAY:

Scripture presents the word of God in two complementary expressions — *Logos* and *Rhema.*

The Logos refers to the written, eternal word—the complete revelation of God recorded in scripture and personified in Christ Himself (John 1:1). It is fixed, final, and authoritative: the plumb line by which all revelation is measured.

The Rhema refers to the spoken or applied word—when the Holy Spirit quickens the *Logos* to the heart, making a specific truth alive and active in a particular moment (Eph 6:17; Matt 4:4).

The *Rhema* never adds to scripture; it draws from it. **The two are not rivals but reflections of one divine source. The *Logos* is the foundation; the *Rhema* is its living echo in real time.** God's Spirit takes what is written and makes it *present*—transforming text into encounter, knowledge into obedience, and truth into experience.

Thus, when we speak of hearing God's "now word," we honour both the written authority of scripture and the living ministry of the Spirit who still speaks today—always in harmony with the word He first inspired.

CHAPTER 7

Physical & Spiritual Israel: Distinct but not Mutually Exclusive

TWO MEANINGS WITHIN ONE STORY

This chapter builds on Paul's thought, clarifying how ethnic Israel and the community of faith intersect in the biblical narrative.

Paul distinguishes but connects physical and spiritual Israel. When Paul writes, "Not all who are descended from Israel belong to Israel" (Rom 9:6), he distinguishes between biological descent and covenant faith.

- Physical Israel refers to the historical nation descended from Abraham, Isaac, and Jacob.

- Spiritual Israel refers to those—Jew or Gentile—who trust in God's promise and live in covenant faithfulness.

These categories are distinct, but they overlap. Paul's own life, as a Jewish follower of Jesus, sits precisely in that intersection.

Notice that a person can be a child, a parent, a sibling, a cousin, and a spouse — all at the same time. This means that more than one truth can be true at once. Take my wife, for example: she is a mother to our children, yet still a daughter to her parents. She's also a sister, a cousin, a wife, and a friend — all wrapped into one. But notice, she can't be my wife, my sister, my cousin, and my daughter (though some cultures try that!) She can't be all those things to one person, yet she can be all of them at once within the same family. In the same way, Paul's vision of Israel holds two realities together — distinct yet belonging to the same family of faith.

TWO DIMENSIONS OF THE ONE ISRAEL:

Likewise, concerning Romans 9:6 when Paul says, "Not all who are descended from Israel belong to Israel," he's distinguishing *two dimensions* of Israel: The physical nation descended from Abraham, Isaac, and Jacob; and the spiritual people of faith who share in the covenant promises.

But crucially, Paul isn't replacing one with the other. He's saying both realities coexist — two meanings within one story — and sometimes the same people occupy both categories *(like Paul himself)*. That's why the analogy about my wife works, as it demonstrates how seemingly separate identities or roles can coexist without contradiction because it captures *precisely* that tension and harmony: One person, many roles — all true at the same time, but not all to the same person.

This mirrors Paul's logic: One covenant story, two dimensions — both true at the same time, but not identical in function. Just as my wife can be a daughter, mother, and wife within one family, *Israel* can be both physical *(national)* and spiritual *(covenantal)* within one redemptive plan. They're distinct yet connected, different in relationship but unified in purpose.

THE REMNANT AS THE LINK

The faithful remnant embodies their overlap. Throughout scripture a faithful remnant preserves continuity between the nation and the covenant ideal. Elijah's seven thousand who refused to bow to Baal (1 Kings 19:18) prefigure the believing minority Paul calls "a remnant according to grace" (Rom 11:5). This group proves that God has not rejected His people; rather, He sustains faith within them. The remnant connects physical Israel to spiritual Israel across history.

FAITH AND LINEAGE IN TENSION

Heritage and faith coexist within divine grace. Paul's letters maintain a delicate balance. He insists that ancestry alone does not confer righteousness (Rom 2:28–29; Gal 3:7), yet he also affirms the continuing significance of Israel's unique calling (Rom 9:4–5). The tension is not contradiction but mystery: grace redefines belonging without erasing heritage. Covenant identity becomes both inclusive *(open to Gentiles)* and particular *(rooted in Israel's story)*.

A VENN-DIAGRAM VIEW

One might picture two overlapping circles:

- The large circle of physical Israel, the people descended from the patriarchs.

- The intersecting circle of spiritual Israel, those living by faith in the covenant promise.

The overlap — the believing Jewish community — forms the living bridge between the two. Gentile believers enter that overlap by grafting, sharing in the same root of faith. Thus the categories are distinct but not mutually exclusive: each retains integrity while participating in the other's fulfilment.

THE DANGER OF MUTUAL EXCLUSION

A "both-and," not "either-or," perspective prevents arrogance or exclusion. History shows how easily the balance can be lost. Some early Christians severed the circles, claiming that the "church" replaced Israel. Others insisted on ethnic exclusivity. Paul's imagery forbids both extremes. The olive tree remains one organism; to cut off either branch is to damage the whole. The covenant cannot be confined to ethnicity nor detached from it.

ESCHATOLOGICAL CONVERGENCE (RECONCILIATION)

The future of redemption culminates in the **reunion of Israel** and the nations under one covenant Lord. Paul's hope in Romans 11 envisions a future reconciliation in which the distinction between physical and spiritual Israel finds harmony: "If their rejection means the reconciliation of the world, what will their acceptance mean but life from the dead?" (Rom 11:15) The narrative ends not in separation but in unity—God's mercy embracing all.

THEOLOGICAL REFLECTION

Paul's vision of Israel joins distinction with unity—two circles that meet in covenant grace. The physical nation remains the historical vessel of God's promises; the spiritual community of faith becomes their living expression. In Christ, these are not rival realities but related dimensions of one redemptive plan. God's election of Israel endures, and His inclusion of the nations fulfils, not replaces, that calling. The faithful remnant bridges the two, reminding us that the covenant root still nourishes every branch. The story is larger than lineage yet never detached from it—one people of promise, joined by grace, kept by mercy.

THEOLOGICAL IMPLICATION

To honour both physical and spiritual Israel is to affirm the full breadth of God's faithfulness. Covenant continuity guards the Church from pride and Israel from despair. Believers from every nation share in one salvation history, dependent on the same mercy and sustained by the same root. The future God envisions is not division but reconciliation—the convergence of promise and fulfilment in the Messiah who unites all things in Himself.

The covenant with Israel has not been annulled but fulfilled in Christ. The promises made to the nation find their higher and spiritual realisation in Him, and through Him extend to all who believe.

— A. B. Simpson[1]

The Church does not take the place of Israel. Rather, it is joined to the believing remnant of Israel — to form one redeemed people, sharing the same promises and drawing life from the same root.

— Derek Prince[2]

God's plan has always been about family. He chose Israel first to reveal Himself, and through them to invite all nations into covenant relationship. The same Spirit continues to breathe on that story, drawing each generation into His unfolding plan.

— Bill Johnson[3]

Thus, physical and spiritual Israel remain distinct yet inseparable — two expressions of one covenant faithfulness, converging in the Messiah through whom all the families of the earth are blessed.

❖

CHAPTER 8

The Olive Tree
of Covenant Mercy

PAUL'S METAPHOR OF CONTINUITY

This chapter focuses on Paul's olive tree metaphor in Romans 11 — one of the richest images of covenant unity and divine faithfulness in all of scripture.

The olive tree represents the single covenant rooted in God's promise. In Romans 11 Paul searches for language strong enough to express both God's judgment and mercy toward His covenant people. He turns to an agricultural image his audience would understand: the cultivated olive tree. The metaphor captures the tension of pruning and growth, loss and renewal. For Paul, the tree itself represents the single covenant story of God and Israel—alive, rooted, and fruitful across generations.

THE ROOT AND THE BRANCHES

Natural and wild branches share one life-giving root. "If the root is holy, so are the branches" (Rom 11:16). The root symbolises the patriarchal covenant—God's promises to Abraham, Isaac, and Jacob. **Holiness flows from divine election, not from human virtue.** The natural branches are the Jewish people, those who belong to the covenant by birthright. Some of these branches have been broken off through unbelief, yet the root remains alive and nourishing. The covenant foundation endures even when individuals or generations waver.

THE WILD SHOOTS GRAFTED IN

Gentile inclusion occurs through grafting, not replacement. Paul's audience in Rome included many Gentile believers. To them he writes: "You, though a wild olive shoot, were grafted in among the others and now share in the nourishing sap from the olive root" (Rom 11:17).

Gentile inclusion is not the planting of a new tree but the surprising act of grafting into the existing one. The metaphor reveals both generosity and dependence: the new branches thrive only because they share in Israel's life-giving root.

THE WARNING AGAINST ARROGANCE

Arrogance severs; humility sustains. Paul immediately adds a pastoral caution: "Do not be arrogant toward the branches... Remember it is not you who support the root, but the root that supports you" (Rom 11:18). "Do not boast over the [broken] branches and exalt yourself at their expense..." (11:18 AMP) "...There's no reason to boast... you owe your life to the root... (11:18 TPT)

This warning addresses a perennial temptation—the tendency for later believers to see themselves as replacing earlier ones. *(Which is right where we are at in this generation yet again. This comes around, every cycle!)* And in Paul's logic, such pride severs the very connection that sustains life. **Faith demands humility toward the history through which grace has come.**

THE MYSTERY OF GOD'S PURPOSE

God's mysterious plan culminates in universal mercy and renewed unity. The apostle's meditation leads him to a "mystery" (Rom 11:25-26): Israel's partial hardening is temporary, allowing time for Gentile inclusion, after which God will restore His people. The imagery suggests divine artistry—pruning and grafting that eventually yield a unified, fruitful tree. The goal is mercy, not division. Every cut and graft serves the gardener's final design: "And so all Israel will be saved."

MERCY AS THE FINAL WORD

Paul concludes with a doxology of astonishment: "For God has consigned all to disobedience, that He may have mercy on all" (Rom 11:32). The olive tree becomes a living parable of mercy's triumph over unbelief. Both Jew and Gentile depend on the same grace; both contribute to the fullness of the covenant story. In the end, the unity of the tree reflects the faithfulness of the gardener.

THEOLOGICAL REFLECTION

The olive tree remains one—rooted in covenant mercy, sustained by divine faithfulness, and pruned for greater fruitfulness. Paul's image captures the unity of God's redemptive purpose: one covenant purpose, many promises; one root, many participants. The Gardener's steady hand ensures that pruning is never rejection but preparation for renewal. The grafted branches of the nations draw life from the same covenant root that sprang from Abraham's promise. In this living tree, judgment and mercy, Israel and the nations, holiness and grace all converge in one divine purpose that testifies: **God has not cast away His people.**

THEOLOGICAL IMPLICATION

The olive tree calls every believer to humility and gratitude. Gentiles are not a new planting but recipients of grace that first flowed through Israel's story. It is *God's* covenant faithfulness—not human constancy—that carries the heritage of redemption. Pride severs; humility connects. The divine plan still aims at restoration.

> God is more than ready to graft back in the natural branches when they turn from clinging to their unbelief to embracing faith. For if God grafted you in, even though you were taken from what is by nature a wild olive tree, how much more can he reconnect the natural branches by **inserting them back into their own cultivated olive tree!**
>
> Rom 11:23-24 TPT

When the natural branches are welcomed back, the whole tree will flourish under one Lord. Mercy is the final word, and unity its fruit. Mercy is God's ecosystem—every branch, old or new, lives by the same life. The Church thrives only as she honours the root that carries her, as Bill Johnson says here:

Mercy flows like a river from the heart of God. When we stay connected to our roots in His goodness, that mercy keeps us alive and fruitful. Cut off from that flow, we begin to wither. Honour keeps us connected to the source.
— Bill Johnson[1]

God's dealings with Israel are a picture of His dealings with His Church. The same covenant faithfulness which will yet restore the natural branches operates now in the salvation of sinners from among the Gentiles.
— Charles H. Spurgeon[2]

The olive tree represents God's people. The root is God's covenant with Abraham, Isaac, and Jacob. The natural branches are Israel; the wild branches are believers from the nations. The Gentiles are not grafted in instead of Israel, but among them, sharing the same life from the same root.
— Derek Prince[3]

Thus, the olive tree stands as a living witness to covenant mercy—its root unbroken, its branches renewed, its fruit proclaiming that God's faithfulness endures for ever.

❖

CHAPTER 9

The Israel of God

THE CONTEXT IN GALATIA

This chapter will look at Paul's phrase in Galatians 6:16 — "Israel of God" — and explore how it has been interpreted, often misunderstood *(becoming the proof-text for replacement ideas)* and how it fits into the larger covenant story that we've been building here. Included is the covenant logic regarding one family of faith that includes *both* Jew and Gentile; with practical implications such as humility, shared vocation, and mutual blessing.

Paul's phrase "the Israel of God" concludes his defence of faith over boundary-keeping. Paul closes his letter to the Galatians with a short blessing that has generated long debate: "Peace and mercy be upon all who walk by this rule, and upon the Israel of God" (Gal 6:16). The phrase comes at the end of a letter written to congregations in Asia Minor struggling over identity.

Some teachers insisted that Gentile believers must undergo circumcision to belong fully to God's people. Paul argues instead that what defines the covenant community is faith expressed through the Spirit, not adherence to the boundary markers of the Law. Against that background, his benediction gathers both groups—Gentile and Jewish believers—under one blessing.

POSSIBLE READINGS OF THE PHRASE

It names the covenant community defined by trust in God's promise. Scholars have long debated whether "the Israel of God" refers only to believing Jews or to the entire community of faith. The grammar allows either reading, yet Paul's argument through the letter favours an inclusive sense: the phrase sums up the new creation community that lives by faith. Still, inclusiveness does not erase distinction. Paul never denies the continuing existence of ethnic Israel; he simply insists that belonging to the covenant is determined by trust in God's promise rather than lineage.

FAITH AS THE CRITERION OF BELONGING

The expression does not cancel ethnic Israel but transcends exclusivity. Throughout Galatians Paul identifies Abraham's true children as those who share his faith: "Know then that it is those of faith who are the sons of Abraham" (Gal 3:7).

This principle unites Jew and Gentile without denying their different histories. The Israel of God, therefore, is not a replacement nation but a description of covenant membership defined by faith. It is Israel renewed from within, expanded to include the nations through the Messiah.

THE RISK OF MISINTERPRETATION

Later "replacement" interpretations misread Paul's intent. In later centuries the phrase was lifted from its context to justify the idea that the Church had superseded Israel entirely. This "replacement" reading contradicts Paul's larger teaching in Romans 9–11, where he insists that God has not rejected His people and that the Gentiles depend on Israel's root. A balanced interpretation holds both truths: the people of God now include believing Gentiles, yet the historical Israel remains beloved for the patriarchs' sake.

ONE FAMILY, MANY BRANCHES

The true Israel is the renewed family of faith through whom God's mercy reaches the world. Paul's vision harmonises with his olive-tree metaphor. All who live by the Spirit share in the same covenant life; they are part of the one people God promised to Abraham. The Church is therefore not a "new Israel" but the renewed Israel, the covenant community extended to the nations. **Its identity is relational — grounded in God's mercy — rather than national or institutional.**

Sadly, as with so many biblical truths, language can blur or even misrepresent the reality. In a similar way, the term *Christian nationalist* is often used in a derogatory way. Yet it would be far more accurate — and far less charged — to speak of a *Christian who loves their nation*. The difference is not trivial; the connotation changes everything.

PRACTICAL IMPLICATIONS

Understanding the "Israel of God" as a community of faith invites humility and gratitude. **It prevents Gentile arrogance and Jewish exclusion alike.** It also restores the missional dimension of election: the renewed people of God exist to bear witness to the covenant Lord in word and deed. Paul's blessing of "peace and mercy" thus becomes a call to **live out reconciliation — the unity of Jew and Gentile in the Messiah of Israel.**

THEOLOGICAL REFLECTION

"The Israel of God" expresses Paul's vision of one redeemed family defined by faith, not lineage. It gathers believing Jews and Gentiles into the same covenant mercy, without dissolving their distinct identities. The phrase does not rename the Church as "the new Israel," but recognises the Spirit-born community that participates in Israel's covenant through the Messiah. It is Israel renewed from within — faith responding to promise, grace uniting what history divided. In this family, the patriarchal blessing reaches its fulfilment: peace and mercy resting upon all who walk by faith.

THEOLOGICAL IMPLICATION

When grace breaks dividing walls, it does not erase identity; it redeems it. The Spirit gathers many branches into one living house, every stone fitted together in love. Including the things that make us different, but which — under grace — become part of divine harmony rather than division.

Rightly understood, "the Israel of God" rebukes pride and restores purpose. It reminds Gentile *(non-Jewish)* believers that they stand by mercy, not merit, and assures Israel that God's covenant affection endures. The true sign of belonging is not boundary but belief — the obedience of faith working through love. To belong to *the Israel of God* is to live as agents of reconciliation: a people formed by covenant, filled by the Spirit, and joined in one calling to bless the nations.

Andrew Murray's theology reflects that our union with Christ makes us as believers sharers *("heirs")* in the divine life and blessing originally promised to Abraham. In other words, faith makes us heirs, *not rivals.* The blessing given to Abraham was a seed meant to multiply, not to exclude:

> *The life that is in the Vine is the life of love. The Spirit that flows through it is the Spirit of love. He that abideth in Me and I in him, the same bringeth forth much fruit. The fruit is love. Love to God and love to men. In the vine each branch lives not for itself, but for all; the life of each is the life of all.*
>
> — Andrew Murray[1]

> *Unity is not conformity; it's the harmony of diversity submitted to one purpose — the glory of God. The Holy Spirit doesn't erase our distinctives (our God-given differences); He redeems them. Grace doesn't make us all the same; it makes us one.*
>
> — Bill Johnson[2]

> *The Israel of God is not a title transferred but a family enlarged; the promises fulfilled, not forfeited.*
>
> — Derek Prince[3]

Thus, *"the Israel of God"* is the living testimony of covenant mercy — many peoples, one faith; many branches, one root; many promises, one Redeemer whose peace and mercy rest upon all who believe.

CORRECTLY UNDERSTANDING THE TERM: *"THE ISRAEL OF GOD"*

Through the centuries this single phrase — *"the Israel of God"* (Gal 6:16) — has been lifted from its context and used to argue that the Church has replaced Israel. That reading turns Paul's benediction into a boundary, whereas he meant it as a bridge. His blessing of "peace and mercy" falls upon *all* who walk by faith — Jew and Gentile alike — without cancelling the distinct calling of *ethnic* Israel.

Paul's use of *"Israel of God"* affirms — two truths held together — throughout scripture: the covenant people of Israel remain beloved for the Father's sake (Rom 11:28), and the nations are welcomed into that same mercy through faith in the Messiah. The phrase therefore speaks of **inclusion without erasure, fulfilment without forfeiture.**

> My beloved brothers and sisters, I want to share with you a mystery concerning Israel's future. For understanding this mystery will keep you from thinking you already know everything. A partial and temporary hardening to the gospel has come over Israel, which will last until the full number of non-Jews has come into God's family. And then God will bring all of Israel to salvation!
>
> The prophecy will be fulfilled that says: "Coming from Zion will be the Savior, and he will turn Jacob away from evil. For this

is my covenant promise with them when I forgive their sins."
Now, many of the Jews are opposed to the gospel, but their
opposition has opened the door of the gospel to you who are
not Jewish.

Yet they are still greatly loved by God because their ancestors
were divinely chosen to be his. And when God chooses someone
and graciously imparts gifts to him, they are never rescinded.
You who are not Jews were once rebels against God, but now,
because of their disobedience, you have experienced God's
tender mercies.

And now they are the rebels, and because of God's tender
mercies to you, you can open the door to them to share in and
enjoy what God has given to us! Actually, God considers all of
humanity to be prisoners of their unbelief, so that he can unlock
our hearts and show his tender mercies to all who come to him.

Rom 11:25-32 TPT

When rightly understood, *"the Israel of God"* protects
the unity of the body and the integrity of God's promises.
It reminds us that divine faithfulness is wide enough to
embrace both the root and the branches, the remnant and the
grafted, until the whole tree rejoices in the Gardener's mercy.

❖

CHAPTER 10

Israel's King
& The Kingdom of God

THE COVENANT EXPECTATION OF A KING

This chapter shows how Jesus' kingship fulfils the covenant promises to Israel and extends them to the nations, tying together the themes of covenant, kingdom, and fulfilment.

Israel's covenant anticipated a perpetual Davidic king. From Israel's earliest history, kingship was tied to covenant. God's promise to David formed the heart of Israel's royal theology: "I will raise up your offspring after you... and I will establish the throne of his Kingdom forever" (2 Sam 7:12–13).

This covenant created an enduring hope that God's rule would one day be embodied in a righteous Davidic king.

The prophets built on this promise, envisioning a reign of justice, peace, and worldwide blessing (Isa 9:6-7; Jer 23:5-6; Zech 9:9-10).

THE ANNOUNCEMENT OF THE KINGDOM

Jesus' announcement of the Kingdom fulfils those promises. When Jesus begins His public ministry, His first declaration is, "The Kingdom of God is at hand; repent and believe the good news" (Mark 1:15).

These words assume the prophetic background. Jesus is not introducing a new idea but announcing that the long-awaited reign of God promised to Israel has arrived in Him. The "good news" (euangelion) was royal language in the ancient world — a proclamation of a king's victory. In Israel's story it signals the arrival of the promised King.

HISTORICAL AND CONTEXTUAL NOTE:

The word εὐαγγέλιον (euangelion) — "good news" or "glad tidings" — is Koine Greek, the common language of the Eastern Mediterranean in the first century — the primary language of the New Testament, alongside some Aramaic expressions and occasional Latin terms.

However, in the wider Greco-Roman world, "euangelion" was used for royal or imperial proclamations — for example, when a new emperor ascended the throne or when a major military victory was achieved. Jesus and the apostles were reclaiming that imperial word, declaring that the true King — not Caesar — had won the victory and established His reign.

THE NATURE OF THE KINGDOM

The Kingdom transforms hearts yet remains grounded in history. **Jesus redefines the Kingdom not as territorial power but as God's rule manifested in transformed lives.** His miracles, parables, and acts of compassion reveal the Kingdom's character: mercy over domination, service over status, healing over exclusion. Yet this transformation is not abstractly "spiritual." It fulfils the covenant promise that God would restore His people and renew creation. The Kingdom is both present in Jesus' ministry and future in its consummation.

THE MESSIAH OF ISRAEL AND THE NATIONS

The Messiah of Israel becomes the Redeemer of all nations. The title "Messiah" *(Christos)* means "Anointed One." In Israel it referred to the anointed king from David's line. Jesus fulfils that expectation but broadens its reach: He is not only Israel's King but Lord of all creation. The Magi who come from the East and the centurion who confesses His lordship foreshadow the universal scope of His reign. The King of Israel becomes the King of the nations — the fulfilment of the Abrahamic promise.

THE CROSS AS CORONATION

The cross is the paradoxical throne of the true King and paradoxically Jesus' enthronement occurs through suffering. The inscription above the cross — "Jesus of Nazareth, King of the Jews" — **intended as mockery, becomes theological truth.** The crucifixion unites covenant loyalty and royal authority: the King lays down His life for His people. In resurrection, God vindicates Him as Lord and Christ (Acts 2:36). The Kingdom's power is revealed not in conquest but in self-giving love.

THE ONGOING MISSION OF THE KINGDOM

The mission of the Church extends His rule until its final consummation. After the resurrection, the disciples ask, "Lord, will you at this time restore the kingdom to Israel?" (Acts 1:6) Jesus replies that the times and seasons belong to the Father but immediately commissions them to bear witness "in Jerusalem, Judea, Samaria, and to the ends of the earth" (Acts 1:8).

Restoration and mission are intertwined: the Kingdom is restored as its message spreads. Every act of witness extends the reign of Israel's King into new territory of human life and culture.

THE FINAL CONSUMMATION

The New Testament closes with a vision of the Kingdom fully realised: "The kingdoms of this world have become the Kingdom of our Lord and of His Christ, and He shall reign forever and ever" (Rev 11:15).

Here, the promises to Israel and the hopes of all nations converge. The same Davidic King who was born in Bethlehem now reigns over all creation. The covenant with David finds its eternal completion in the universal sovereignty of Christ.

THEOLOGICAL REFLECTION

- The Kingdom is rooted in Israel's story but open to the world.

- Jesus fulfils royal prophecy by embodying servant leadership.

- The cross reveals kingship through love rather than force.

- The mission of the Church continues the expansion of that Kingdom.

- The final consummation unites heaven and earth under one King.

The Kingdom of God reveals the covenant faithfulness of Israel's King fulfilled in Christ and extended to the nations. Every promise to David finds its completion in the risen Messiah, whose throne was established—not by human conquest—but by divine victory through the cross.

In Jesus, divine sovereignty takes on human form; His crown is of thorns before it is of glory. The gospel is therefore not a new message but the ancient royal announcement that God reigns—first over Israel, then through Israel's King over all creation. The Kingdom remains rooted in history yet transcendent in scope: personal in the heart, global in mission, and eternal in destiny.

THEOLOGICAL IMPLICATION

To confess Jesus as King is to enter the covenant story and to live as citizens of His reign. The Kingdom is not built by might or politics but by transformed hearts that manifest the justice, mercy, and humility of the King. Israel's promised ruler now governs through His Spirit, calling the nations to obedience born of love.

The Church extends His reign not by replacing Israel but by reflecting His rule—serving, healing, and reconciling—until the day when every crown is cast before His throne and every tongue confesses that **Jesus Christ is Lord.** Christ's reign is both present and active, not postponed:

> *The King has not abdicated His throne. He is still healing the sick, saving the lost, and pouring out His Spirit. The Kingdom of God is not coming someday in the sweet by and by; it is here now in the hearts of those who yield to Him.*
>
> —Rodney Howard-Browne[1]

> *The Gospel of the Kingdom is not just words—it comes with the power of the King. When Jesus is enthroned in the heart, His Kingdom comes with power to change the world around us.*
>
> —Reinhard Bonnke[2]

> *The Kingdom of God is not advanced by carnal policies nor by worldly wisdom. It is built up by prayer, enlarged by the preaching of the word, and strengthened by faith. The Church marches on her knees.*
>
> —E. M. Bounds[3]

Thus, the story of Israel's King becomes the story of the world's Redeemer—His covenant throne unshaken,

His Kingdom advancing, and His reign destined to unite heaven and earth under one everlasting Lord.

❖

CHAPTER 11

The Universal Lordship
Of Our Messiah

FROM COVENANT KING—TO COSMIC LORD

This chapter expands the vision of Jesus' kingship beyond Israel's borders to the entire created order, showing how His reign fulfils both covenant and creation purposes.

This points to the universal reign of Israel's Messiah. Which means that Jesus' kingship expanded from covenantal to cosmic scope; a progression — of Jesus' reign — as reflected precisely in the New Testament: *The Messiah of Israel is the Lord of heaven and earth (cf. Phil 2:9–11; Col 1:15–20)*. This is an important trajectory from promise to fulfilment, from national covenant to global redemption:

- **Covenant King**—speaks of His kingship within Israel's covenant story *(rooted in Abraham, David, and the promises to Israel).*

- **Cosmic Lord**—shows the universal scope of His reign—Lord over all creation, not just over Israel.

The New Testament presents a striking development of Israel's royal hope. The same Jesus who fulfils the promises to David is also declared "Lord of all" (Acts 10:36). The royal Messiah becomes the universal ruler, not through conquest but through resurrection. **In Him the covenant with Israel and God's purpose for creation converge.** The Lord who called Abraham and ruled from Zion is now recognised as the one through whom and for whom all things were made.

THE COSMIC DIMENSION IN PAUL'S LETTERS

Paul portrays Christ as creator, sustainer, and reconciler of all things. Paul's Christology expands the scope of redemption to encompass the universe: "All things were created through Him and for Him... and in Him all things hold together" (Col 1:16–17). "That in the fullness of time God might unite all things in Christ, things in heaven and things on earth" (Eph 1:10).

Here, the "Kingdom of God" takes on cosmic proportions. The Messiah's reign restores not only human relationships but the harmony of creation itself. Sin fractured the cosmos; the risen Christ heals it.

THE LORD OF HEAVEN AND EARTH

When early believers proclaimed "Jesus is Lord," the statement carried political and theological weight. In the

Roman world, "Lord" *(kyrios)* was a title reserved for emperors and gods. The confession that Jesus holds this title signals allegiance to a sovereignty that transcends earthly power. The crucified Jew from Nazareth reigns over heaven and earth—an assertion that redefines authority and power at every level.

THE COSMIC SCOPE OF RESURRECTION

The resurrection renews the fabric of creation. Meaning that the resurrection was more than the reversal of death; it is the renewal of creation's order. Paul calls Jesus "the firstborn from the dead" (Col 1:18), implying that His rising inaugurates a new reality in which decay and futility no longer have the final word. The same Spirit that raised Jesus now works to redeem all creation from bondage (Rom 8:19–21). Cosmic lordship thus involves cosmic restoration.

WORSHIP AS THE LANGUAGE OF ACKNOWLEDGMENT

Worship and stewardship express recognition of His lordship. The hymns embedded in early Christian writings reflect this expanded vision. Philippians 2:9–11 portrays every knee in heaven, on earth, and under the earth bowing to Jesus, and every tongue confessing His lordship. Worship becomes the fitting response of all creation to its true King. The cosmic Christ is not a philosophical abstraction but the personal Lord who reconciles heaven and earth through love.

IMPLICATIONS FOR CREATION AND HUMANITY

The cosmic dimension of the Messiah's reign restores meaning to creation itself. Environmental care, justice, and compassion flow from acknowledging His lordship. The same King who rules galaxies also values sparrows and lilies. To serve Him is to affirm that the material world matters and that redemption includes the physical as well as the spiritual.

ESCHATOLOGICAL COMPLETION

The new creation fulfils God's covenant purpose in universal harmony. Revelation envisions the climax of this cosmic reign: "Then I saw a new heaven and a new earth… and the throne of God and of the Lamb shall be in it" (Rev 21:1; 22:3). The story that began in a garden ends in a city where God dwells with humanity. The Davidic Messiah's rule becomes universal; covenant faithfulness has renewed creation itself.

THEOLOGICAL REFLECTION

- The Messiah of Israel is also Lord of creation.
- His resurrection inaugurates the renewal of the cosmos.
- Worship acknowledges His universal sovereignty.
- Divine lordship calls humanity to stewardship, not exploitation.
- The goal of history is the union of heaven and earth under one Lord.

The covenant story of Israel widens into a cosmic (*universal*) horizon in the risen Christ. The same Lord who reigned from Zion now rules the galaxies. His resurrection is not merely the triumph of life over death, but the renewal of creation itself. Through Him all things were made; through Him all things are restored. The promise to Abraham and the purpose of creation converge in one Person: Jesus, the Messiah of Israel and the Lord of heaven and earth. Worship, therefore, becomes the language of alignment—humanity and creation joining to acknowledge the sovereignty of the One in whom all things hold together.

THEOLOGICAL IMPLICATION

The cosmic lordship of Christ redefines both authority and responsibility. **To confess *Jesus is Lord* is to live under His reign in every sphere**—personal, relational, and creational. Stewardship becomes worship when care for God's creation, justice, and mercy flow from reverence for the Creator-King. The same hands that shaped the stars also bear the marks of covenant love. His universal sovereignty calls His people to reflect His character—to rule by serving, to lead by loving, and to tend the world as citizens of His Kingdom. The goal of redemption is not escape from creation but its renewal under one Lord and one covenant of peace.

The substance of Derek Prince's teaching in two separate chapters of his book, *(chapter 11 "Israel's Restoration and the Return of the Lord" and chapter 12 "The Church and the Coming Kingdom")* he wrote the following:

> *Redemption will reach as far as the fall has spread its effects. God's mercy, revealed first to Abraham, will embrace all nations... When Israel is restored and Messiah reigns from Jerusalem, the whole earth will enter into peace and righteousness. The curse will be lifted from creation, and*

harmony will be restored between man and nature.

—Derek Prince[1]

God's sovereignty is the attribute by which He rules His entire creation (cosmos), and to be sovereign, God must be all-knowing, all-powerful, and absolutely free. The reasons for all that He does lie in Himself.

—A. W. Tozer[2]

The Kingdom of God is ever increasing. It will fill the whole earth with His glory. The same Spirit that fills the believer will one day fill the nations.

—Rodney Howard-Browne[3]

Thus, the covenant King revealed in Israel now reigns as the cosmic Lord of creation—the Alpha and Omega of all history, the centre where heaven and earth meet, and the fulfilment of God's eternal purpose of love.

❖

CHAPTER 12

The New Jerusalem

THE END OF THE STORY, NOT ITS ERASURE

This chapter brings the narrative arc to its climax, showing how the story that began with Abraham and Israel ends in a renewed creation and a united people under the reign of the Messiah

This is important to understand, but it is spiritually discerned — not in an esoteric or mystical sense, but as truth drawn directly from the word of God — for *"the testimony of Jesus is the spirit of prophecy" (Rev 19:10).*

For example, I once read a thread of comments on a random Instagram post about the New Jerusalem descending out of heaven as the Bride of Christ (Rev 21:2). Many of those commenting were completely ignorant of this biblical theme. They were furious with the preacher who had simply read directly from his bible — a true *rock of offence* (Isa 8:14; Rom 9:33; 1 Pet 2:8). They did not comprehend biblical covenant, nor did they have any understanding of prophetic imagery — the mystery of the gospel (Eph 3:4–6) — and so they took great offence.

To be clear, the New Jerusalem is both a **place** and a **people** — a city and a bride. It represents the redeemed community of God, joined together in perfect union with Him. When John describes the city "coming down out of heaven from God," he is not speaking of an abstract vision but of the fulfilment of God's covenant promises — heaven and earth reunited, God dwelling among His people once more (Rev 21:3). The imagery is layered but consistent: a holy city, a purified bride, and a restored creation. **It is both literal in hope and symbolic in expression, revealing that God's purpose has always been relational — to dwell with His people and make all things new.**

NOT ESCAPE BUT RENEWAL

Revelation's final vision unites heaven and earth in covenant fulfilment. **The bible closes not with escape from the world but with renewal.** John's vision in Revelation 21–22 reveals continuity between creation, covenant, and consummation: "Then I saw a new heaven and a new earth… and I saw the holy city, New Jerusalem, coming down out of heaven from God" (Rev 21:1–2).

The imagery gathers the entire biblical story into one scene. The covenant begun with Abraham and renewed through David reaches its fulfilment as heaven descends to earth, uniting divine presence and redeemed creation.

A CITY BUILT ON COVENANT FOUNDATIONS

The city's foundations merge Israel's tribes and the apostles of the Lamb. John's description fuses the symbols of Israel and the Church:

> It had a great, high wall with twelve gates, and at the gates twelve angels, and on the gates were the names of the twelve tribes of the sons of Israel... The wall of the city had twelve foundations, and on them were the twelve names of the twelve apostles of the Lamb.
>
> Rev 21:12, 14

The city's architecture itself preaches theology. The twelve tribes and the twelve apostles stand together, forming a single structure. The people of God are one, joined by shared covenant faith and divine mercy. Israel and the nations no longer stand in tension; they are complementary stones in the same foundation.

THE PRESENCE OF GOD RESTORED

Divine presence replaces all distance and mediation. In Eden, humanity lost direct fellowship with the Creator. In the New Jerusalem, that fellowship is restored in fullness: "Behold, the dwelling of God is with humanity. He will dwell with them, and they will be His people" (Rev 21:3).

The tabernacle and temple, symbols of mediated presence, give way to unbroken communion. There is no need for sun or temple, "for the glory of God gives it light, and the Lamb is its lamp" (Rev 21:23). What was promised through the prophets—God's Spirit within His people—finds visible completion.

THE HEALING OF THE NATIONS

The nations' healing completes the Abrahamic blessing. The river of life flowing from the throne nourishes "the tree of life," whose leaves are "for the healing of the nations" (Rev 22:2). This image fulfils the Abrahamic covenant: through his seed, blessing reaches every family of the earth. The New Jerusalem is not parochial; it is universal. The nations bring their glory into it, a sign that diversity is preserved and sanctified within God's Kingdom. The covenant purpose that began with Israel's election now embraces all creation.

THE MOUNT OF OLIVES AND
THE RETURN OF THE KING

The story returns to its beginning — the Creator dwelling with His people forever. So the story circles back to geography sanctified by history. The prophets foresaw that the Messiah would return to the Mount of Olives (Zech 14:4), the very place of His ascension (Acts 1:11–12). The physical and the spiritual, heaven and earth, meet in one restored reality. The covenant God who walked with Abraham and spoke through Moses now dwells among His people forever.

LIFE IN THE ETERNAL CITY

The closing vision is marked by abundance, not austerity. Water, light, and fruitfulness symbolise life without curse. Service replaces striving: "His servants will serve Him; they will see His face" (Rev 22:3–4). This is the true sabbath of history — creation at rest under its rightful King.

THEOLOGICAL REFLECTION

- Fulfilment, not Replacement: The New Jerusalem completes the story of Israel and the Church; it does not begin a new one.

- Unity in Diversity: Tribes and apostles together express the wholeness of God's people.

- Presence Restored: God's dwelling with humanity is the goal of covenant history.

- Creation Renewed: The final vision affirms the goodness of the material world made new.

- Hope Realised: Every promise of blessing finds its "Yes" in the Lamb who reigns.

The New Jerusalem is the climax of the covenant story — the meeting place of heaven and earth, of promise and fulfilment. What began in Eden's garden concludes in the city of God, where divine presence and redeemed creation dwell together forever. The same covenant God who called Abraham now brings His purpose to completion: the dwelling of God with humanity restored in radiant permanence. The Lamb's light replaces every shadow, and worship becomes the atmosphere of existence itself.

Here, the story of Israel and the Church is no longer unfolding but complete. The foundations bear the names of the tribes and the apostles, declaring that covenant faith and divine mercy have formed one eternal household. The Holy City is both literal and symbolic — the place and the people of God, the bride adorned for her husband. Every thread of prophecy, every covenant promise, and every act of redemption culminate in this unveiled glory.

THEOLOGICAL IMPLICATION

The vision of the New Jerusalem calls believers to live now as citizens of that city. Hope becomes holiness, and expectation becomes endurance. The same Spirit who will one day fill that city already dwells within His people, shaping their lives into living stones. The redeemed community thus becomes a preview of the world to come—embodying reconciliation, purity, and worship in the present age.

To fix our eyes on the New Jerusalem is not escapism but alignment. It shapes our ethics, our worship, and our mission. We live as those preparing for a world restored, not destroyed—"for the new heaven and new earth, renewed by the covenant faithfulness of God." The covenant faithfulness that will one day illuminate every street of the eternal city is the same grace that sustains our daily walk now.

Heaven will not be a foreign place for the believer, for the life of heaven has already begun in the heart where Christ dwells (Col 1:27). Yet the New Jerusalem is not an inward vision or metaphor—it is a real city that will descend "out of heaven from God, prepared as a bride adorned for her husband" (Rev 21:2). Its radiance is the outshining of divine glory, the visible meeting place of heaven and earth, where "the tabernacle of God is with men, and He will dwell with them" (Rev 21:3).

The eternal city is not distant; it is descending. Heaven's pattern is breaking into creation until righteousness and peace fill the earth (Isa 32:17; 65:17). The New Jerusalem is the consummation of all covenants — the home of the redeemed, the fulfilment of every promise, and the throne of God and of the Lamb (Rev 22:3). It is heaven's answer to earth's long cry for restoration, "the city which hath foundations, whose builder and maker is God" (Heb 11:10).

> *The New Jerusalem will be the eternal home of God's redeemed people. There, the purposes of God for Israel, the Church, and the nations will find their perfect fulfilment. God Himself will dwell among His people, and His glory will fill all creation.*
>
> —Derek Prince[1]

> *The invasion of God's Kingdom into this world is not to take us out of here, but to bring His reality into every part of culture. Heaven is invading earth.*
>
> —Bill Johnson[2]

> *Heaven is not only a place to which we go; it is a life that begins here below. The Spirit brings down heaven into our hearts, for where the Spirit of Jesus dwells, there heaven has begun.*
>
> —Andrew Murray[3]

Thus, the New Jerusalem reveals the covenant brought to its perfection — the presence of God restored, the promises fulfilled, and creation renewed in the everlasting light of the Lamb.

❖

CHAPTER 13

The Church's Obligation to Israel

PAUL'S PRINCIPLE OF GRATITUDE

This chapter explores how the Gentile church relates to Israel in light of God's covenant faithfulness, and how humility, gratitude, and prayer should shape that relationship.

Gentile believers share in Israel's blessings and therefore owe gratitude and service. In his letter to the Romans, Paul makes a simple yet profound statement: *"For if the Gentiles have come to share in their spiritual blessings, they ought also to be of service to them in material things" (Rom 15:27).*

This verse captures the heart of the Church's posture toward Israel. Gentile believers have received the revelation of God, the scriptures, the Messiah, and the Spirit through Israel's covenant story. Gratitude, therefore, becomes obligation—the response of those who have inherited grace through another's faithfulness (*God's own faithfulness through Israel's story*).

REMEMBERING THE ROOT

The Church's identity is rooted in Israel's covenant history. The early Church understood itself as grafted into Israel's olive tree, not planted in its own soil. Forgetting this root risks spiritual amnesia. The Church owes to Israel not only its sacred texts but its very understanding of covenant, sin, redemption, and worship. To neglect or disdain the people through whom these gifts came is to misunderstand the character of the God who gave them.

THE ERROR OF ARROGANCE

As mentioned in an earlier chapter, arrogance toward Israel contradicts the gospel of mercy. Paul's warning in Romans 11—*"Do not be arrogant toward the branches"*—remains relevant. Throughout history, parts of the Church drifted into pride and contempt, viewing Jewish unbelief as justification for persecution or neglect. Such attitudes contradict the gospel's own logic of mercy. The Church's vocation is to provoke Israel to jealousy (Rom 11:11), meaning to inspire holy desire for the blessings found in the Messiah, not to fuel division or resentment.

THE MINISTRY OF PRAYER AND BLESSING

Prayer and compassion express solidarity with God's people. Psalm 122:6 commands, "Pray for the peace of Jerusalem."

For believers in every age, this prayer expresses hope for the fulfilment of God's promises. To pray for Israel's peace is to pray for reconciliation, justice, and spiritual renewal. It is also an act of solidarity with the story through which one's own salvation has come. Intercession becomes participation in God's redemptive plan.

WITNESS THROUGH COMPASSION

Gratitude takes tangible form in acts of compassion. Supporting Jewish communities, standing against antisemitism, and cultivating genuine friendship are natural expressions of covenantal faith. The gospel calls the Church not to paternalism *(spiritual superiority)* but to partnership, recognising the shared heritage of grace. Service and empathy testify that the same God who chose Israel continues to work through her destiny.

THEOLOGICAL FOUNDATIONS OF OBLIGATION

The obligation is theological as well as moral and ethical: one root, one hope, one mission and the relationship is reciprocal, woven into the fabric of God's saving plan.

- **Shared Covenant:** The Church partakes of promises first given to Israel.

- **Shared Hope:** Both await the final restoration when all Israel will be saved.

- **Shared Mission:** The nations bless Israel, and Israel blesses the nations.

HUMILITY AS A SIGN OF TRUE FAITH

Humility and gratitude mark the authentic Church. At its core, the Church's responsibility to Israel reflects humility before divine sovereignty. The same mercy that grafted Gentiles into the olive tree keeps Israel within reach of restoration. The Church stands as evidence of God's mercy, not as a judge of Israel's unbelief. Paul's final doxology in Romans 11 reminds believers that the mystery of election leaves no room for pride — only awe.

THE PATH FORWARD

Mutual blessing anticipates the final reconciliation under the Messiah's reign. A renewed awareness of this obligation can heal old divisions. By remembering the Jewish roots of the faith, honouring the continuity of God's covenants, and rejecting every form of antisemitism, the global Church, the body of Christ, bears witness to the faithfulness of the God of Abraham. The ultimate goal is mutual blessing — the unity of Jew and Gentile in worship of the same Lord.

THEOLOGICAL REFLECTION

The Church's calling toward Israel is not sentimental — it is covenantal. Gratitude, humility, and prayer arise from recognition, not obligation alone. The Gentile believers have been grafted into a story not their own, yet one into which they are graciously invited. Every blessing the Church enjoys has its roots in Israel's history and God's promises to the patriarchs.

The Church therefore stands not as a successor but as a steward—called to honour the root that sustains her and to reveal the mercy that grafted her in. The measure of spiritual maturity is not superiority but humility: to love what God loves, to bless whom He has blessed, and to remember the covenant that endures. In every generation, true faith bows before divine faithfulness.

THEOLOGICAL IMPLICATION

To bless Israel is not optional; it is covenantal. When the Church forgets her root, she loses her fruit. The Church's obligation to Israel calls believers to tangible expressions of covenant awareness—through prayer, compassion, and honour. To pray for Jerusalem's peace is to align with God's redemptive plan. To stand against antisemitism is to stand with the God of Abraham. To bless Israel is to participate in the very promise through which the nations are blessed.

This humility shapes both evangelism and eschatology. Again and again, we must repeat that the Church's mission is not to replace Israel, but to walk beside her until the fullness of redemption comes. As Paul wrote, *"Salvation has come to the Gentiles to provoke Israel to jealousy" (Rom 11:11).*

God's covenant faithfulness to Israel is His signature upon history. What He began with Abraham, He will complete through Christ for all nations. The Church's witness, therefore, must be radiant with gratitude—not pride—for *gratitude should ever express itself in love,* displaying the same mercy that first reached her. Blessing Israel isn't sentimental—it's covenantal. **The Church was grafted in, not begun anew;** to forget Israel is to forget our root:

God signed His name across the pages of history through His covenant with Abraham. Through Israel the nations would see His faithfulness. What He began in Abraham finds its fulfilment in Christ, for the Gospel is the continuation of that covenant mercy to all peoples.

—Reinhard Bonnke[1]

The debt of the Gentile world to the Jewish people is immense. Out of them came the Book, and the prophets, and above all, our Lord Himself. Gratitude should constrain us to love them, and to seek their good.

—Charles H. Spurgeon[2]

Blessing Israel is not a sentimental duty; it is part of God's covenant plan. The Church owes her existence to the root from which she sprang. Forgetting that root is spiritual amnesia.

—Reinhard Bonnke[3]

Thus, the Church's obligation to Israel is not a burden but a blessing—an invitation to share in God's own fidelity, to honour His promises, and to mirror His mercy until Jew and Gentile rejoice together in the restoration of all things.

❖

CHAPTER 14

The Error of
Replacement Theology

DEFINING THE CONCEPT

This chapter deals with one of the most consequential missteps in church history: the idea that the Church replaced Israel in God's purposes. It traces the origins, effects, and theological corrections to that view, while maintaining balance.

"Replacement theology," also known as super-sessionism, is the belief that the Church has permanently displaced Israel as God's covenant people. According to this view, because Israel rejected the Messiah, God rejected Israel, transferring His promises entirely to a new, primarily Gentile community. The term "Israel" is then reinterpreted to mean "the Church," and the Old Testament covenants are seen as void or fulfilled in such a way that they no longer apply to the Jewish people.

While this idea arose gradually, it profoundly shaped Christian thought for centuries — and often with devastating ethical and social consequences.

EARLY ROOTS & HISTORICAL DEVELOPMENT

Historically, it arose from tension between Jewish and Gentile believers. The earliest followers of Jesus were all Jews who saw faith in Him as the culmination of Israel's story, not its cancellation. However, as the gospel spread into the Gentile world and relations with the synagogue grew tense, theological distance widened. By the second century, thinkers like Justin Martyr and later Augustine began to describe the Church as the "true Israel," often interpreting Israel's continuing existence as a symbol of unbelief rather than of God's faithfulness.

This shift coincided with political realities: as Christianity became associated with empires, the Jewish people — stateless and dispersed — were increasingly marginalised. Over time, replacement theology provided the theological justification for social and political exclusion.

THEOLOGICAL CONSEQUENCES

The doctrine undermines the reliability of divine promise. Supersessionism alters the very character of God's faithfulness. **If God's eternal promises to Israel can be revoked, the security of any divine promise becomes**

uncertain. Paul's entire argument in Romans 9–11 stands against this: "The gifts and the calling of God are irrevocable" (Rom 11:29).

The logic of covenant demands continuity. The New Covenant fulfils and expands previous covenants; it does not nullify them. A theology that severs this continuity risks portraying God as changeable or unreliable — precisely what scripture denies.

ETHICAL CONSEQUENCES

It produced centuries of moral and social harm. Historically, replacement theology fostered contempt toward the Jewish people. When theology identifies a living people as rejected by God, persecution becomes easier to rationalise. The tragic outcome was centuries of discrimination, forced conversion, and violence in the name of Christian faith. These acts contradict the very gospel that proclaims mercy and reconciliation. The correction of supersessionism is therefore not only doctrinal but moral.

THE BIBLICAL CORRECTIVE

Scripture presents a different pattern. Taken together, these passages below affirm one *continuous* story of **covenant fidelity:**

- God's covenant with Israel remains intact even amid disobedience (Jer 31:35–37).

- The inclusion of Gentiles fulfils the promise that through Abraham's seed all nations would be blessed (Gen 12:3).

- Paul's metaphor of grafting (Rom 11) allows for expansion without replacement.

- The New Jerusalem unites Israel's tribes and the apostles of the Lamb (Rev 21:12–14).

THE CALL FOR A RENEWED UNDERSTANDING

Scripture maintains continuity through covenant fulfilment, not cancellation. There is a need for modern theology to solidly recognise that the Church does not replace Israel but participates in Israel's redemptive calling through faith in her Messiah. Gentiles are joined to Israel's promises; Israel's identity is not erased but fulfilled. A view that restores the unity of scripture and the moral coherence of divine faithfulness.

To be abundantly clear, honouring Israel is **not about exalting a nation** above others; it's about recognising and exalting God's covenant faithfulness and divine nature. And that the promises made to Abraham are the foundation of God's redemptive plan for the world.

THE PATH TO RECONCILIATION

Correcting this error restores the integrity of God's faithfulness and the unity of His people. Rejecting replacement theology invites repentance and renewal. It calls Christians to honour their Jewish roots, to combat antisemitism, and to see **Israel's continuing existence as a sign of God's unbroken covenant.** Dialogue and mutual respect become acts of obedience to the same God who called both Israel and the nations into His mercy.

THEOLOGICAL REFLECTION

- God's faithfulness to Israel underwrites His faithfulness to all.

- The Church is grafted into, not substituted for, the covenant people.

- Supersessionism distorts both biblical theology and Christian ethics.

- True covenant theology affirms continuity, humility, and hope.

Replacement theology strikes at the heart of God's revealed character. If His covenant with Israel could be revoked, then no promise would be secure. But scripture reveals a God whose faithfulness outlasts rebellion and whose mercy transcends generations. The God who chose Israel has not changed His mind. The cross is not the sign of rejection but of redemption — where covenant justice and covenant mercy meet.

The Church's proper posture is not triumph but thanksgiving. Every Gentile believer stands by faith upon the same promises first spoken to Abraham. The root still nourishes the branches; the covenant still upholds the tree. To deny Israel's place in God's plan is to misunderstand the nature of grace itself. For grace never erases — it restores, fulfils, and expands.

THEOLOGICAL IMPLICATION

Rejecting replacement theology is not an academic correction; it is repentance — a turning of the heart toward the faithfulness of God. The Church's future health depends on recovering her covenant memory. To love Israel is to love the God who bound Himself to her. To pray for her peace is to align with His eternal purpose.

Theological humility, moral integrity, and prophetic clarity all flow from this recognition: that God's word cannot fail. The same faithfulness that preserves Israel sustains the Church and secures the world's hope. Thus, continuity with Israel is not optional — it is essential to a true understanding of redemption history. **When we honour Israel, we are not *idolising* a nation *(which is sometimes the accusation)*;** we are acknowledging God's covenant faithfulness. His promises to Abraham are the anchor of *global* redemption. It is in our own best interest!

> *The Church does not take the place of Israel. Rather, we who are Gentile believers are grafted into the stock of Israel to share its life and its promises...* **God has not finished with Israel.** *The Church and Israel each have their appointed roles in His eternal purpose.*
>
> — Derek Prince[1]

> *Any theology that teaches that God has cast away His ancient people will soon teach that He can cast away His new people also. But His covenant stands fast forever.*
>
> — Charles H. Spurgeon[2]

> *When God makes a covenant, He puts Himself in it. His integrity is involved in its fulfilment. He cannot go back on His word.*
>
> — E. W. Kenyon[3]

Thus, the *correction of replacement theology* is not merely doctrinal—it is an act of worship *(doxological)*. To rediscover God's unbroken covenant with Israel is to return to awe before His faithfulness. It calls the Church to humility, repentance, and praise—to marvel again at the God whose mercy never ends, whose promises never fail, and whose covenant with Israel still stands as the sure guarantee of hope for the nations, *(every nation)*.

❖

CHAPTER 15

The Peace of Jerusalem

A COMMAND AND A HOPE

This chapter shows how Jesus' kingship fulfils the covenant promises to Israel and extends them to the nations, tying together the themes of covenant, kingdom, and fulfilment.

Praying for Jerusalem's peace aligns believers with God's redemptive purpose. The psalmist's exhortation has echoed for three millennia: **"Pray for the peace of Jerusalem: 'May they prosper who love you'"** (Ps 122:6).

This simple command carries deep theological weight. Jerusalem is more than a city; it is the heart of Israel's covenant story, the symbol of God's dwelling among His people. To pray for her peace is to align oneself with God's purpose for reconciliation, justice, and restoration. It is both intercession and confession — an acknowledgment that true peace is the fruit of divine faithfulness.

THE BIBLICAL MEANING OF PEACE

Shalom signifies wholeness and justice, not mere calm. The Hebrew word *shalom* means more than the absence of conflict; it conveys wholeness, harmony, and flourishing — the integration of all things under God's covenant reign. In prophetic vision, Jerusalem's peace is inseparable from righteousness: *"The work of righteousness will be peace, and the effect of righteousness, quietness and confidence forever"* (Isa 32:17).

David himself recognised that the source of such peace and greatness was not human strength but divine character, declaring, *"Your gentleness has made me great"* (2 Sam 22:36; Ps 18:35). This covenantal gentleness reveals the heart of Israel's true King — whose righteousness establishes peace, and whose tender dealings with His people bring restoration, not replacement.

In the New Covenant, this same peace finds its fulfilment in the Messiah, of whom it is written, *"He Himself is our peace (εἰρήνη, eirēnē), who has made both one and has broken down the middle wall of separation"* (Eph 2:14). Paul's use of *eirēnē* deliberately echoes the Hebrew *shalom*, revealing the continuity of God's covenant purposes. The peace of the Messiah flows from His faithfulness to Israel's promises and extends through Him to the nations — uniting Jew and Gentile under one Shepherd and one righteous rule.

To pray for Jerusalem's peace, therefore, is to seek the coming of God's Kingdom in its fullness, when justice and mercy embrace.

JERUSALEM IN SALVATION HISTORY

Jerusalem embodies the continuity of God's covenant story. Her role in scripture traces the full arc of redemption and helps shape the destiny of the nations. Jerusalem's story, like Israel's, moves from promise to fulfilment, from division to restoration:

- It was the city of David, where the covenant of kingship took shape.

- It was the site of the temple, where God's presence dwelt amongst His people.

- It was the city where prophets wept and where Jesus was crucified and raised.

- It will be, according to prophetic promise, the focal point of renewal: "At that time they will call Jerusalem 'The Throne of the Lord,' and all nations shall gather to it" (Jer 3:17).

We use these four major points consistently to solidify and honour Israel's covenant role — a God-given position — that stands firmly against replacement interpretations:

1. Davidic covenant *(kingship),*

2. Temple *(presence),*

3. The Messiah's suffering and resurrection *(redemption),*

4. Prophetic fulfilment *(restoration and rule).*

THE SPIRITUAL AND THE EARTHLY

The heavenly and earthly Jerusalems converge in the final restoration. The New Testament carries Jerusalem's meaning forward without discarding its earthly significance. For example, the letter to the Hebrews speaks of a "heavenly Jerusalem" (Heb 12:22), and Revelation envisions the city descending from heaven (Rev 21:2). The two are not opposites but dimensions of the same reality: the earthly city anticipates the perfected one, and the heavenly city affirms the destiny of creation redeemed. The hope of peace is therefore both spiritual and historical—a longing for God's reign to be manifested in the real world.

THE CHURCH'S PARTICIPATION

For believers among the nations, praying for Jerusalem's peace means embracing solidarity with Israel's story and hope. It calls for repentance where the Church has fostered hostility, and for active goodwill toward the Jewish people. It also means living as agents of peace in one's own context—embodying reconciliation, humility, and mercy as signs of the Kingdom to come. To bless Jerusalem is to bless the God who chose her for His purposes.

THE PEACE THAT COMES THROUGH THE KING

The Messiah Himself is the source and guarantee of true peace. Ultimately, Jerusalem's peace is bound to the person of the Messiah. The prophets foresaw a ruler who would "speak peace to the nations" (Zech 9:10). In Christ, peace is both gift and calling: "He Himself is our peace, who has made both one and has broken down the dividing wall" (Eph 2:14).

The shalom for which believers pray begins in reconciliation with God and extends outward to the reconciliation of peoples. Every prayer for Jerusalem's peace anticipates the day when "nation shall not lift up sword against nation" (Isa 2:4).

THE ESCHATOLOGICAL VISION

Revelation's final vision fulfils Psalm 122's longing: the New Jerusalem descends, radiant with the glory of God, and "the leaves of the tree are for the healing of the nations" (Rev 22:2). The city of peace becomes the dwelling of God with humanity. The covenant with Abraham, the promise to David, the outpouring of the Spirit — all find their consummation in this vision of universal harmony. The story ends where it began: with divine presence and human peace united.

LIVING TOWARD PEACE AND RESISTING JEW HATRED

The Church's task is to live as agents of reconciliation until that peace fills the earth (2 Cor 5:18–20; Isa 11:9). Until that day, believers are called to be witnesses of the coming Kingdom through acts of reconciliation and justice (Matt 5:9; Mic 6:8). To pray for Jerusalem's peace is to live in anticipation of it — to embody shalom in our communities, families, and nations (Ps 122:6; Rom 14:19). Each act of mercy and understanding is a small reflection of the final restoration God has promised (Isa 65:17–19; Rev 21:1–4), and it is precisely why we must resist Jew-hatred from ever infiltrating the Church (Rom 11:18; Gen 12:3).

A bird has two wings; with one it cannot fly — or be truly aerodynamic. Likewise, prayer and action must go hand in hand, for *faith without works is dead (Jas. 2:17)*. So we have a biblical responsibility, not only to PRAY for the peace of Jerusalem but also TO ACT accordingly (Ps 122:6; Heb 13:16).

THEOLOGICAL REFLECTION

- The peace of Jerusalem is both local and cosmic *(universal)* — a sign of God's plan for creation.

- True peace arises from righteousness and reconciliation through the Messiah.

- Praying for Jerusalem's peace expresses gratitude for the covenant's root.

- The hope of New Jerusalem unites believers in anticipation of God's dwelling among humanity.

The peace of Jerusalem is the melody of redemption fulfilled. From Abraham's tent to David's throne, from Calvary's cross to the heavenly city, God's covenant faithfulness has been moving toward this harmony — shalom that heals creation and reconciles the nations. The peace we pray for is not political ease but divine order restored: righteousness and mercy embracing, heaven and earth united under one King.

Jerusalem stands as both symbol and substance — the visible reminder that God's promises remain rooted in history yet reach to eternity. Her peace foretells the restoration of all things. To love her is to love the covenant that birthed salvation; to pray for her peace is to long for the reign of the Prince of Peace Himself.

THEOLOGICAL IMPLICATION

To pray for the peace of Jerusalem is to align with the heartbeat of God. It is to participate in His covenant plan through intercession, compassion, and active pursuit of reconciliation. This prayer is not passive—it summons believers to embody the peace they seek. Every act of justice, mercy, and unity becomes a foretaste of the coming Kingdom.

The Church's witness must therefore combine devotion and action—two wings of the same calling. Prayer without compassion becomes empty words; action without prayer becomes human striving. But together they manifest covenant partnership: heaven's purpose expressed through human obedience. The peace of Jerusalem, then, is not merely Israel's destiny—it is the destiny of creation under its rightful King.

When you pray for the peace of Jerusalem, you are praying for the completion of God's purpose for the entire human race. You are praying for the establishment of God's Kingdom on earth.

—Derek Prince[1]

Peace is not the absence of trouble, but the presence of Christ. When He reigns in Jerusalem, the whole earth shall rest.

—Andrew Murray[2]

Prayer prepares the atmosphere for revival; intercession for Jerusalem prepares the world for His coming. When Zion prays, heaven moves.

—E. M. Bounds[3]

Thus, the call to *pray for the peace of Jerusalem* gathers the entire story into one act of hope—a prayer that becomes prophecy, a longing that becomes fulfilment, a faith that waits for the day when the Prince of Peace reigns from Zion and His glory fills the earth.

They Say...

They say Israel is **done**
her covenant broken,
her calling lost,
her promise revoked.

But Heaven does not agree.

The covenant still stands —
written by the finger of God,
sealed in His faithfulness,
unchanged by time,
untouched by man's unbelief.

Replacement Theology —
man's theory, not God's truth —
dares to rewrite
what the Eternal has decreed.

Yet the Word of the Lord remains:
unchanging,
unbroken,
everlasting.

The same God who scattered Israel
is gathering her again.

Her imperfection does not nullify His perfection.
Her failure does not silence His faithfulness.

What He began in Abraham,
He is completing in Christ.

— Poem by Jennifer Pateman 2025

❖

CHAPTER 16

Final Words on:
The Delegitimisation of Israel

TOP QUESTION: IS THE MODERN STATE OF ISRAEL PART OF THE ABRAHAMIC COVENANT?

This is one of the most important questions of our time. And the short answer is a resounding YES. It is biblically accurate in essence and well within a sound, Spirit-filled interpretation of scripture to say that the modern State of Israel is definitively and definitely part of the Abrahamic Covenant.

However, there are those today — very prominent figures — who are claiming that the current State of Israel has NOTHING to do with Biblical Israel! And like most influencers online they like to speak with such authority as if they actually *know* what they are talking about! Unfortunately they don't. And perhaps ignorantly are aligning themselves with and being used by the "the accuser of the brethren" who slanders them day and night (Rev 12:10).

Let's break it down carefully and theologically one last time:

1. THE MODERN STATE OF ISRAEL AND BIBLICAL ISRAEL

The claim that "the current State of Israel has nothing to do with Biblical Israel" is contrary to scripture. Because God's covenant with Abraham, Isaac, and Jacob *(Israel)* was eternal and unconditional regarding the land:

> I will establish My covenant between Me and you and your descendants after you throughout their generations for an everlasting covenant, to be God to you and to your descendants after you. And I will give to you and to your descendants after you... all the land of Canaan, for an everlasting possession; and I will be their God.
>
> Gen 17:7–8 AMP

The Hebrew word for everlasting—עוֹלָם *(olam)*—means perpetual, without end. The prophet Jeremiah affirms that the covenant with Israel cannot be revoked:

> Thus says the Lord, who gives the sun for a light by day... "If these ordinances depart from before Me," says the Lord, "then the seed of Israel also shall cease from being a nation before Me forever."
>
> Jer 31:35–36 KJV

That is an explicit divine guarantee that Israel's nationhood would remain.

2. THE REBIRTH OF ISRAEL IN PROPHECY

The re-establishment of Israel in 1948 fulfils multiple prophetic passages:

Isaiah 66:8 (NLT) — "Who has ever seen anything as strange as this? ... Can a nation be born in a single day?" This vividly anticipates Israel's miraculous rebirth in one day — 14 May 1948.

Ezekiel 36–37 — Ezekiel foresaw both the physical restoration *(return to the land)* and the spiritual restoration *(breath of the Spirit into the dry bones)*. The first has already begun; the second will culminate at the Messiah's return.

Derek Prince consistently taught that the restoration of Israel to their land was the single greatest prophetic sign that the time of the Gentiles was drawing to a close.

The return of the Jewish people to their own land is the single most important prophetic sign that we are approaching the close of this age. Nothing in all history has so clearly and dramatically fulfilled the prophecies of scripture as the restoration of Israel. It is a sure sign that the times of the Gentiles are drawing to their close, and that the personal return of the Lord Jesus is near.

— Derek Prince[1]

Again, this understanding aligns with Christ's words in Luke 21:24, that *"Jerusalem will be trampled on by the Gentiles until the times of the Gentiles are fulfilled,"* and with Paul's prophetic insight in Romans 11:25, that *"blindness in part has happened to Israel until the fullness of the Gentiles be come in."*

Prince's interpretation thus situates Israel's modern restoration not as a political anomaly but as a divine countdown marker in God's covenant timetable.

3. ACCUSING ISRAEL AND "THE ACCUSER OF THE BRETHREN"

Revelation 12:10 points to the devil who is called "the accuser of our brethren", whose goal is to slander and undermine God's COVENANT PEOPLE. When people—especially Christian voices—join in the slander or delegitimisation of Israel, they inadvertently echo that same spirit of accusation.

This warning is widely attributed to Charles Spurgeon: *"I never read of a single instance in scripture of any man who persecuted Israel and prospered after it."* In essence, Spurgeon cautioned that those who set themselves against Israel never ultimately prospered, observing that scripture offers no example of anyone who persecuted God's covenant people and escaped divine judgment.[2]

4. FINAL BIBLICAL CONCLUSION

The modern State of Israel is not a coincidence of history but a continuation of God's covenant purpose with the Jewish people. Those who deny this either misunderstand the covenants or have been influenced by replacement theology, which scripture itself refutes. The mystery of Israel is central to God's purposes for the world. We cannot understand prophecy or redemption without understanding Israel.

Spurgeon's warning echoes the unchanging covenant principle first spoken to Abraham: *"I will bless those who bless you, and I will curse him who curses you" (Gen 12:3 NKJV).* Again, this divine decree has NEVER been revoked; it forms the moral and spiritual law of how nations and individuals fare in relation to Israel.

The prophet Zechariah reinforces this when God declares, *"He who touches you touches the apple of His eye" (Zech 2:8 AMP).* **Scripture therefore leaves no ambiguity — God identifies Himself with His covenant people. To oppose Israel is, in effect, to oppose the covenant-keeping God who chose her.**

History repeatedly confirms this truth: empires have risen against Israel and fallen, yet the people of the covenant remain, a living testimony that, *"the gifts and the calling of God are irrevocable" —* Rom 11:29 (AMP see 11:1-2, 25–29).

The detractors of Israel always point to the fact that its a NEW covenant. That the OLD replaces the NEW. But as Andrew Murray once said,

> *There are two covenants, one called the Old, the other the New. ... The Old Covenant was one dependent on man's obedience, one which he could break, and did break (Jer 31:32). The New Covenant was one which God has engaged shall never be broken; He Himself keeps it and ensures our keeping it: so He makes it an Everlasting Covenant.*[3]

❖

Epilogue

FAITHFULNESS REMEMBERED

The story of Israel and the nations concludes not with rivalry but with worship. The same covenant God who called Abraham now gathers the families of the earth to share in one table of mercy. The Church's faith and Israel's calling meet in the peace of Jerusalem — the symbol of God's eternal fidelity.

> For from Him and through Him and to Him are all things. To Him be glory forever. Amen.
>
> Rom 11:36

From beginning to end, the story has been one of faithfulness. The God who called Abraham, sustained Israel through exile, and fulfilled His promises in the Messiah, remains the same today. His purpose has never changed — to bless all nations through the covenant He initiated and to dwell among His people in peace.

The arc of scripture reveals no interruption in this design. The story of scripture flows without break or breach: the covenant made with Abraham, carried through Isaac and Jacob, continued through Moses, and crowned in David reaches its completion in the New Covenant of grace. The Church, gathered from every nation, partakes in Israel's calling without dissolving her identity. The same root still nourishes every branch—natural and grafted alike.

The hope of the believer rests, therefore, on the unwavering reliability of God. If He has been faithful to Israel through centuries of trial, He will be faithful to all who trust His word. Every covenant, every promise, every act of mercy finds its "Yes" in the Messiah.

> For no matter how many promises God has made, they are "Yes" in Christ. And so through him the "Amen" is spoken by us to the glory of God.
>
> 2 Cor 1:20 NIV

In this, Paul is declaring that every covenant promise God ever made—to Abraham, to David, to Israel—finds its affirmation *("Yes")* in Jesus the Messiah, and its agreement *("Amen")* through the faith of believers. Again, this doesn't erase or replace the covenants; it confirms them in their Messiah, who is the living embodiment of God's faithfulness (Rom 15:8).

WHOSOEVER WILL—COVENANT GRACE FOR *ALL* NATIONS

To recap, the covenants remain rooted in Israel, but the invitation is open to all. God's promises are yes and amen in Jesus (2 Cor 1:20), and their reach extends to **"whosoever will."** The Kingdom expands, not by replacement, but by inclusion—through faith in Israel's Messiah.

The promises and covenants of God are steadfast, fulfilled, and confirmed in the Messiah of Israel. Again, in Him, every divine promise finds its "Yes and Amen" (2 Cor 1:20). Yet the wonder of grace is that this covenant mercy, first revealed through Israel, is now extended to all who believe— "For **whosoever** shall call upon the name of the Lord shall be saved" (Rom 10:13; Joel 2:32). From the beginning, God's heart has been for the nations, that through Abraham's seed "all families of the earth shall be blessed" (Gen 12:3).

The invitation remains open: **"Whosoever will,** let him take the water of life freely" (Rev 22:17). Thus, the Gospel is not the cancellation of Israel's calling, but its expansion—the covenant faithfulness of God offered to Jew and Gentile alike through one Redeemer, Jesus the Messiah.

A UNIVERSAL INVITATION & DIVINE FIDELITY

So, to pray for the peace of Jerusalem, to hope for the renewal of creation, and to live as agents of reconciliation—these are not separate tasks but expressions of the same faith. The story that began with a single call, "Go from your country," ends with a universal invitation: "Come, everyone who thirsts."

Between those two commands, stretches the entire drama of redemption, held together by divine fidelity.

In that faithfulness the Church stands, and in that faithfulness the world will one day find its peace.

The steadfast love of the Lord never ceases; His mercies never come to an end; they are new every morning; great is Your faithfulness.

Lam 3:22–23

❖

Note on Referenced Authors

SPIRITUAL DEPTH AND FIDELITY TO SCRIPTURE

The authors referenced throughout this work were not selected for novelty or reputation, but for their spiritual depth, fidelity to scripture, and proven fruit. Though differing in era and style, they share one conviction: **God keeps His covenants and His word.**

Their writings, spanning centuries and traditions, affirm the continuity of God's redemptive purpose, the faithfulness of His character, and the error of any theology that would sever the Church from her Jewish root. From the devotional depth of **Andrew Murray** and the prophetic clarity of **Derek Prince**, to the evangelical conviction of **Charles Spurgeon** and the Spirit-empowered vision of **Reinhard Bonnke, Bill**

Johnson, and **Rodney Howard-Browne** — each bears witness to the same God whose promises to Israel and the Church remain irrevocable.

These voices, though diverse in expression, converge in reverence for scripture, dependence on the Holy Spirit, and confidence in the reliability of God's word. Their inclusion here honours that enduring testimony — voices across generations united in proclaiming that the promises of God are "Yes and Amen" in Christ. Their insights do not replace the bible's authority but amplify its message: the faithfulness of God resounding from Abraham to the nations, and from covenant promise to universal fulfilment.

❖

Quotes:
From Notable Public Figures

BILL MAHER: "HAMAS HAS TO BE DESTROYED"

Sometimes its refreshing to see celebrities and influencers stand up for Israel. Speaking on Club Z recently Bill Maher had this to say in Israel's defence:

Verbatim excerpt (from Club Random / Club Z clips):

Hamas has to be destroyed. This is not as complicated as people make it. Yes, we're all concerned about what happens after Hamas is destroyed the day after. We don't know. I assume Israel has something in mind. They're not stupid people.

But the idea that you can let an entity that has attacked you five times, after you gave the land back, gave the land back in 2005, they could have done anything they wanted with it. It could be Dubai now, if they had chosen, but they chose to take the money, that much of the world donated to them and spend it not on their own people (who they use as human shields), but to buy bombs and rockets and build tunnels and just attack Israel endlessly.

Five times since 2005, including the most recent one on October 7th of last year [2023], and they have avowed over and over again — it's in their charter — it's in their public statements. 'We will continue to do this.' That's what from the river to the sea means. 'We get all of it, you disappear...'

So the question is, should Hamas be destroyed? And most people agree it should be. Then the next question is, how do you do it? Well, I'll tell you... we don't know how that's going to be accomplished. I assume the Israeli Defence Force has a little more idea than we do.

And also, I trust Israel more than any other country in the world, because they have a track record of at least trying to not kill civilians. That is their history."

— Bill Maher[1]

BILL MAHER: ISRAEL DID NOT STEAL ANYBODY'S LAND (REGARDING WHO GOT THERE FIRST, APARTHEID AND OCCUPATION)

Uh, I would submit that Israel did not steal anybody's land. This is another thing I've heard the last couple of weeks. Words like "occupiers" and "colonisers" and "apartheid," which I don't think people understand the history there. The Jews have been in that area of the world since about 1200 B.C. Way before the first Muslim or Arab walked the earth. A thousand years before. I mean, Jerusalem was their capital. Okay, so if it's just about who got there first, it's not even close.

— @jewsforyeshua[2]

FOOTNOTE: ON BILL MAHER

Bill Maher's comments carry weight with many today because he isn't given to group-think. A genuine *contrarian*, he questions cultural consensus rather than echoing it. Partly Jewish, Maher is a secular American comedian, political commentator, and television host known for sharp wit and fearless candour. Though broadly liberal, he stands apart — progressive on issues like free speech and civil rights, yet openly critical of ideological extremes on both left and right. More than an entertainer, Maher belongs to the Voltairean tradition of free thinkers who challenge dogma to protect honest discourse.

Like Voltaire *(François-Marie Arouet, 1694–1778)*, famed for the maxim *"I disapprove of what you say, but I will defend to the death your right to say it,"* Maher represents a modern voice for reasoned dissent — insisting that truth is strengthened, not silenced, through open debate. **Though we differ with many of his views (*of course!*) yet on Israel he speaks with refreshing clarity and moral courage to a culture reluctant to hear it. He is, quite simply, an anomaly in our times.**

JONATHAN CAHN:
REGARDING THE MODERN STATE OF ISRAEL

Jonathan Cahn, who identifies as a Messianic Jewish prophetic teacher and author, upholds the authority of scripture, and the continuing covenantal significance of Israel, and the Messiahship of Jesus *(Yeshua)*. His teachings align with Spirit-filled, prophetic, covenantal theology, not replacement theology. Cahn is mostly known for revealing biblical "mysteries" that connect ancient prophecy to modern events, and specifically that the covenant promises to Israel remain active. That understanding Israel's role is key to grasping God's overall redemptive and prophetic plan. *(See his book The Harbinger II [Charisma House, 2020].)*

Recently on instagram he pointed out that many today are asking: **"Is the modern state of Israel part of the Abraham Covenant?"** Which we have attempted to answer in this particular book. In addition, the major false claims — echoing across the internet — are as follows: "If Israel isn't made up of mostly believers, we don't need to bless them" *(emotional ignorance!)* The biggest one that resonates today is: "If we don't always agree with their government *(specifically the IDF and Bibi Netanyahu)* we shouldn't bless them."

On Instagram, in a reel titled *Understanding the Abrahamic Covenant and Israel's Place in It,* he addresses whether Israel's national status is dependent on belief. Here he directly deals with such claims by saying:

Here's the problem with that: Israel has existed in the form of a nation or state, a kingdom of polity, in one way or another from ancient times in the bible. So if God applied the Abrahamic Covenant back then to the nation or state of Israel or Judah, then he certainly applies it to the nation or state of Israel now.

Israel in the days of Solomon wasn't following God, – most of the people, – but it was still Israel, and all God's promises still applied. Israel in the days of Jeremiah – same thing – wasn't following God (most of them), but it never stopped being Israel, and the promises didn't stop either.

Israel in the days of Messiah, Jesus, (Yeshua), was under the Herods, who were ungodly evil leaders, but it never stopped being Israel, and the promises of God were never revoked.

So first, it doesn't matter whether they believe or not yet. It doesn't matter what its government is – if one agrees or disagrees with any policy. You don't have to agree with it, any more than you have to agree with every American government policy, or your own family, or your parents, or your children.

That has nothing to do with it. Every nation is imperfect. You stand with your family, your parents, your children, you bless them, you support them, and so with Israel.

And just as much as the kingdom of Judea was Israel, and the days of Messiah, and the kingdom of Judah, in the days of Jeremiah, and the kingdom of Israel in the days of Salomon, you know, there's more to Israel in that there are children of Israel still living in the nations, as in ancient times, but that does not in any way take away the fact that Israel is Israel.

—Jonathan Cahn[3]

MENTOR TO CHARLIE KIRK, DR FRANK TUREK: ON CAN CHRISTIANS SUPPORT ISRAEL AS AN APOSTATE NATION TODAY?

Dr Frank unpacks God's reason for choosing Israel-and what that means for believers now.

Question: *"Okay, my question for you today is: Being that we are all made in the image of God, why did God first choose a nation of people out of the whole world to be His chosen people, the Israelites, and second, how can the nation still to this day deny the divinity in the [sic; sacrificial] nature of Jesus Christ, our Lord and Savior?"*

Answer: *"Okay, remember in Deuteronomy, I believe it is, when God says, "I chose you, the Israelites, not because you're the greatest, but you're the smallest of all people, you're the least, and I want to demonstrate my power through you." So when he says, "I'm choosing the Israelites through whom I want to bring the Messiah," He's not saying the Israelites are any better than anyone else. When God says they're chosen, it doesn't mean they're favoured. It just means they were chosen, through which God was going to save the entire world.*

And now you might say, "Well, the nation of Israel now is apostate. They're not believers." Well, I understand that, but let's think back into Old Testament history. In the Old Testament, they were all apostates too!

136

Do you know the nation of Israel, the northern nation, out of, I think, 20 kings or 19 kings, every single one of them was a bad king. Right. Only a few in the Southern kingdom Judah were good kings.

So when people say, **"Well, you know, there's nothing you can support about the modern state of Israel 'cause they're all apostate, if you're a Christian."** *You couldn't support ancient Israel, either, if that was your standard.*

In fact, what is the ongoing theme of the Old Testament? It's just one prophet after another going, "You guys better stop going after other gods, or you're gonna get judged," and they kept getting judged! In fact, this is one reason I know the Old Testament's true.

In fact, Dennis Prager said this — you know, Dennis Prager is a conservative Jewish man, not a Christian — but he said, **"One of the main reasons I know the Old Testament is true is because no people group would ever invent such an embarrassing history of themselves!"**

— Dr Frank Turek[4]

STUART KNECHTLE: A LIGHT TO ALL NATIONS NOT JUST THE JEWS

When the bible teaches that the Jews are the chosen people, it does not mean that Jews are superior to Gentiles. It does not mean that the Jews are God's pets. It simply means that when God wanted to reveal Himself most clearly, He spoke through the Jewish prophets, the Hebrew prophets.

And when He wanted to reveal Himself very clearly, He became a human being, born a Jew. I worship a Jew, which means, obviously, antisemitism is impossible for me as a follower of Jesus Christ, for I worship a Jew as God in human form.

The chosen people were chosen by God to communicate His truth, His love, to the world. The Jewish people were chosen by God through whom He would bring Messiah into the world. **Jesus was born of a Jewish woman, Mary.**

And therefore, the Jewish people are the chosen people in the sense that God chose them to reveal Himself most clearly. **But it does not mean that Jews are superior to Gentiles.** *It means we all are created in the image of God, that God has chosen to speak very clearly to a specific group of people, and He chose to become a human being for you.*

He spoke through Abraham, talking about how his descendants, land and so forth, would be given to him and the Israelites. **But they were to be a light to ALL nations. So it was simply by God's grace that they were chosen.** *Nothing in and of themselves, that they did right or wrong... Clearly, Paul talks about this in Galatians: There's neither Jew nor Gentile, all are created in God's image. So do I celebrate Jerusalem? Absolutely — in the history of it — but* **it was certainly a light to all nations that all would be saved.**

—Stuart Knechtle[5]

CHARLIE KIRK: PRAY FOR THE PEACE OF JERUSALEM (PS 122:6–9 KJV)

(HE WAS CONFLICTED OVER THE GOVERNMENT OF ISRAEL BEFORE HIS DEATH)

But there's a lot of things the Israeli government does that I don't like. **I can name them. The Israeli government has really bad abortion policies. Israeli government has gay pride parades in downtown Tel Aviv. The Israeli government pushed a vaccine on all their people and basically turned Israel into a Petri dish for a vaccine that none of us supported.** *I don't like the fact that the Israeli government mistakenly or unmistakably bombed a church the last couple weeks ago.*

We shouldn't support that. With all that being said, though, Israel looks like a much better country when contrasted with what I said earlier, with Islamic totalitarianism around it. They're not a perfect country, they're not a country that, honestly, we should even talk as much as we do, but we **as Christians should pray for the peace of Jerusalem. That is unmistakable.**

We as Christians should <u>reject Jew hate</u>, and we as Christians to find unity in one thing that we can all agree on, we should seek to bring every Jewish person on the planet to Jesus Christ, because Jesus is the answer.

— @hugomoreno316[6]

Footnote: This is to add context to some things Charlie said before he died about Israel. He was not anti Israel. As a bible believer he knew his position on Israel. Yet was not an apologist for the Israeli government. These were his own words.

CHARLIE KIRK:
ON ANTISEMITISM & GENOCIDE IN GAZA

Question: "Do you support Israel?"

Answer: *"Yes, of course I do. Yes. Everything that Israel does gets so hyper examined through this lens that no other country ever gets held to the standard of, ever. Nobody does anything like Israel. It's easy to say, "Oh, the Jews run everything." If the Jews run everything, why is there so much antisemitism? It is an intentional provocation, and I find it to be repulsive, the over used word genocide, because when you keep on using genocide, you're basically trying to cheapen actual genocides that have happened the last 100 years. You think that Israel is intentionally trying to kill as many people in Gaza as possible? Well, they're not doing a great job with it cause the population keeps on going up! And when you declare War on Israel, expect a fire storm in reaction."*

— @meaningfulminute[7]

RANDOM PERSON:
"WHY WOULD BILLIONS OF CHRISTIANS BELIEVE?"

Why are the Christians supporting Israel or supporting the Jews so much?" Answer: "The Christians that follow the bible, that follow Jesus, that follow our Torah and the New Testament. It says that whoever blesses Israel will be blessed, whoever curses Israel will be cursed, and they

140

*know that the Messiah, their Savior, came from the Jewish people. **It's not us going into a Gentile faith. It's Gentiles being brought into the fold of the people of Israel because of the promises of God to the entire world. The promise to Abraham, when God said, "I will make you a great nation, and through your seed, <u>all the peoples will be blessed,</u> not just the Jewish people, all the people will be blessed.***

They understand that that promise is fulfilled in Yeshua. Why else would billions of Christians around the world and through history believe in the God of Abraham, Isaac, and Jacob? Why?

Why would they give up idol worship? ***Why would they give up being liked and loved by popular culture? Why would they do that?*** *Because of Jesus the Jew, from Nazareth.*

— @jewsforyeshua[8]

INSIGHT:

This points to the Messianic reign of Jesus — the Prince of Peace — when He will rule from Jerusalem (Isa 2:2–4). Reinhard Bonnke often said, **"The gospel began in Jerusalem, and it will finish there."**

> The Lord says: I am returning to Mount Zion, and I will live in Jerusalem. Then Jerusalem will be called the Faithful City; the mountain of the Lord of Heaven's Armies will be called the Holy Mountain… They will be My people, and I will be their faithful and just God.
>
> Zech 8:3–8 NLT

141

FORWARD OR PASS IT ON!

Note: If this book has blessed you, let it bless others. Share it, and let the message bear fruit in someone else's life. *"What you have heard... entrust to... others"* *(2 Timothy 2:2).* Why not sow by gifting a copy, or even placing a bundle in the hands of your home group or church? In this way the truth multiplies and glorifies our Heavenly Father.

A massive Thank You

❖

Endnotes

Chapter 1 The God Who Calls

1. A. W. Tozer, *The Pursuit of God*, p. 11 (Harrisburg, PA: Christian Publications, 1948).

2. Derek Prince, *Foundations for Righteous Living*, ch. 2 "The Grace of God." (New Kensington, PA: Whitaker House, 2001).

3. Charles H. Spurgeon, *The Metropolitan Tabernacle Pulpit* Vol. 28, Sermon No. 1663, "The Effectual Call" (London: Passmore & Alabaster, 1882).

Chapter 2 Israel: Chosen for a Purpose

1. Derek Prince, *The Destiny of Israel and the Church*, p. 41 (New Kensington, PA: Whitaker House, 2007).

2. Charles H. Spurgeon, Sermon No. 1307, "Divine Choice and Human Duty," *The Metropolitan Tabernacle Pulpit*, Vol. 22 (London: Passmore & Alabaster, 1876).

3. A. W. Tozer, *The Pursuit of God*, ch. 1 "Following Hard After God". (Harrisburg, PA: Christian Publications, 1948).

Chapter 3 The Faithfulness of God in Israel's History

1. Derek Prince, *The Destiny of Israel and the Church*, p. 63 (New Kensington, PA: Whitaker House, 2007).

2. Charles H. Spurgeon, *The Metropolitan Tabernacle Pulpit Sermons* Vol. 35, p. 482 ("The Faithfulness of God").

3. A. W. Pink, *The Attributes of God,* p. 60 (Baker Books, 1975 [orig. 1930]).

Chapter 4 Jesus: The Fulfilment, Not the Cancellation

1. A. B. Simpson, *The Christ in the Bible Commentary,* Vol. 4, p. 212 (Christian and Missionary Alliance, 1910).

2. Watchman Nee, *The Normal Christian Life,* p. 126 (Christian Fellowship Publishers, 1957).

3. Benny Hinn, *Blood in the Sand,* p. 97 (FrontLine, 2009).

Chapter 5 Pentecost: The Renewal of Israel

1. Reinhard Bonnke, *Evangelism by Fire,* p. 58 (Full Flame Publications, 1990).

2. Andrew Murray, *The Spirit of Christ,* p. 74 (Marshall Pickering, 1894).

3. E. M. Bounds, *The Power of Prayer,* p. 116 (Fleming H. Revell Co., 1910).

Chapter 6 The Gentile Mission: Grafted In Not Replaced

1. Charles H. Spurgeon, *Metropolitan Tabernacle Pulpit Sermons,* Vol. 33, p. 412 (Sermon No. 1985, "The Olive Tree of Grace") (London: Passmore & Alabaster, 1887).

2. Derek Prince, *The Destiny of Israel and the Church,* p. 87 (Whitaker House, 2007).

3. Watchman Nee, *The Normal Christian Church Life,* p. 129 (Christian Fellowship Publishers, 1939).

Chapter 7 Physical & Spiritual Israel: Distinct but Not Mutually Exclusive

1. A. B. Simpson, *The Christ in the Bible Commentary: Romans,* p. 214 (Christian Alliance Publishing, 1912).

2. Derek Prince, *The Destiny of Israel and the Church,* p. 93 (Whitaker House, 2007).

3. Bill Johnson, *The Resting Place: Living Immersed in the Presence of God,* p. 178 (Destiny Image, 2011).

Chapter 8 The Olive Tree of Covenant Mercy

1. Bill Johnson, *The Resting Place: Living Immersed in the Presence of God,* p. 184 (Destiny Image, 2011).

2. Charles H. Spurgeon, *Metropolitan Tabernacle Pulpit Sermons,* Vol. 33, p. 512 "The Olive Tree of Grace" (London: Passmore & Alabaster, 1887).

3. Derek Prince, *The Destiny of Israel and the Church,* p. 101 (Whitaker House, 2007).

Chapter 9 The Israel of God

1. Andrew Murray, *The True Vine,* p. 82 (Marshall Pickering, 1895).

2. Bill Johnson, *Hosting the Presence,* p. 203 (Shippensburg, PA: Destiny Image, 2012).

3. Derek Prince, Paraphrased from *The Destiny of Israel and the Church,* p. 109 (Whitaker House, 2007).

Chapter 10 Israel's King & The Kingdom of God

1. Rodney Howard-Browne, *The Coming Revival,* p. 119 (Revival Ministries International, 1998).

2. Reinhard Bonnke, *Evangelism by Fire,* p. 72 (Orlando, FL: Full Flame Publications, 1990).

3. E. M. Bounds, *The Weapon of Prayer,* p. 88 (New York: Fleming H. Revell Co., 1916).

Chapter 11 The Universal Lordship Of Our Messiah

1. Derek Prince, *The Destiny of Israel and the Church,* pp. 142-143 (New Kensington, PA: Whitaker House, 2007).

2. A. W. Tozer, *The Knowledge of the Holy,* p. 122 (Harper & Row, 1961).

3. Rodney Howard-Browne, *The Coming Revival,* p. 187 (Revival Ministries International, 1998).

Chapter 12 The New Jerusalem

1. Derek Prince, *The Destiny of Israel and the Church,* p. 214 (New Kensington, PA: Whitaker House, 2007).

2. Bill Johnson, *When Heaven Invades Earth,* p. 162 (Shippensburg, PA: Destiny Image, 2003).

3. Andrew Murray, *The Spirit of Christ,* p. 289 (James Nisbet & Co., 1888).

Chapter 13 The Church's Obligation to Israel

1. Reinhard Bonnke, *Evangelism by Fire,* p. 88 (Full Flame Publications, 1990).

2. Charles H. Spurgeon, *Metropolitan Tabernacle Pulpit Sermons,* Vol. 35, p. 482 "The Faithfulness of God," (London: Passmore & Alabaster, 1889).

3. Reinhard Bonnke, Paraphrased from *Evangelism by Fire,* p. 178 (Full Flame Publications, 1989).

Chapter 14 The Error of Replacement Theology

1. Derek Prince, *The Destiny of Israel and the Church,* pp. 31, 59 (Whitaker House, 2007).

2. Charles H. Spurgeon, *Metropolitan Tabernacle Pulpit Sermons,* Vol. 35, p. 479 ("The Faithfulness of God", Passmore & Alabaster, 1889).

3. E. W. Kenyon, *The Blood Covenant,* p. 17 (Seattle: Kenyon's Gospel Publishing Society, 1949).

Chapter 15 The Peace of Jerusalem

1. Derek Prince, *The Destiny of Israel and the Church,* p. 226 (Whitaker House, 2007).

2. Andrew Murray, Paraphrased from *The Spirit of Christ,* p. 312 (James Nisbet & Co., 1888).

3. E. M. Bounds, Paraphrased from *The Weapon of Prayer,* p. 148 (Fleming H. Revell Co., 1916).

Chapter 16 Final Words on: The Delegitimisation of Israel

1. Derek Prince, *The Key to the Middle East,* (PA: Whitaker House, 2013 ed., pp. 23–24)

2. Paraphrased from C. H. Spurgeon, "The Church of Christ and the House of Israel," sermon #430, 1862.

3. Andrew Murray, *The Two Covenants and the Second Blessing*. (London: James Nisbet & Co., 1898). Chapter II: "The Two Covenants." (Original text available via Blue Letter Bible, public domain reproduction: https://www.blueletterbible.org/Comm/murray_andrew/two/two02.cfm)

Quotes: From Notable Public Figures

1. Bill Maher, remarks in Club Random / Club Z clip (video repost), Instagram reel, accessed October 2025. https://www.instagram.com/reel/DO7lgzlCJR2/?utm_source=chatgpt.com

2. This is jewsforyeshua on instagram maejoggerst515, an account advocating for the release of the hostages - from Oct 7 2023. Accessed Oct 2025

3. @Jonathan.cahn, accessed October 2025. https://www.instagram.com/reel/DNlFP32pElS/?igsh=MTJmYWR0a3lrcXRrZg==

4. @DrFrankTurek Instagram, accessed October 2025. Dr Frank Turek is an American Christian apologist, author, and founder of CrossExamined.org. A mentor to Charlie Kirk, He is best known for: "I Don't Have Enough Faith to Be an Atheist" and his defence of the Christian worldview in public debate. https://www.instagram.com/reel/DP7f3HZjByb/?igsh=ODluNWx2c2tqaTF3

5. @Stuartknechtle accessed October 20 2025. https://www.instagram.com/reel/DQAMQcrkXqb/?igsh=MWgzYzFicHNmOTB3dQ==

6. @hugomoreno316 accessed Oct 2025. Charlie was talking at a convention possibly in a church. It's in the public domain — available on many accounts. Charlie died September 10th 2025

7. Charlie Kirk at Turning Point USA campus gathering. Student question regarding Israel. @meaningfulminute — random source. Jewish Motivation account. Jewish content.

8. @jewsforyeshua accessed Oct 2025

Bible translations

Drs Alan and Jennifer Pateman

are missionaries from the UK,
who at present reside in Tuscany, Italy,
and travel together as an apostolic team. They
are the Founders of Alan Pateman World Missions,
Connecting for Excellence International Fellowship,
LifeStyle International Christian University,
and APMI Publishing/Publications.

*(Please see our website for all profile and
international information, itinerant, conferences
and graduations, etc.)*

www.AlanPatemanWorldMissions.com

❖

To Contact the Authors

Please email:

Alan Pateman World Missions

Email: apostledr@alanpatemanworldmissions.com
Web: www.AlanPatemanWorldMissions.com

*Please include your prayer requests
and comments when you write.*

❖

Other Books on the Endtimes

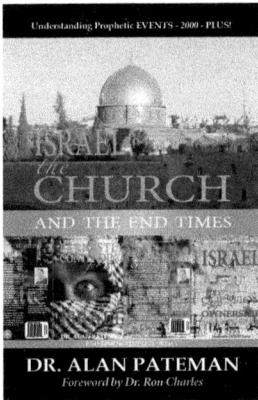

Israel, the Church and the End Times
(complete series)

Dr Alan Pateman's End Times Series not only seeks to bring the reader "up to date" with regard to present day societal eschatological convictions, showing how Israel is in fact, God's chosen instrument that will be used to chart and to instigate fulfilment of these long anticipated end-time events.

He also accurately traces the history of how the Jews through history have been used as God's instrument; how evil forces have for centuries, all the way up to this present time, sought to destroy these people, their mission, their purpose, and their unique position within the overall plan of God; and how the worldwide entrenchment of modern day apostasy, materialism and deception will immediately proceed the realization of these end-times events, anticipated for so many thousands of years.

ISBN: 978-1-909132-77-1, Pages: 448,
Format: Paperback, Published: 2018
Also available in Hardback and eBook format!

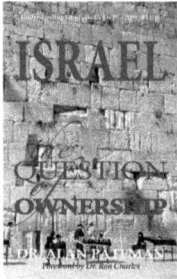

Israel, the Question of Ownership

One thing we can be sure of and is the deciding factor: God has given this land, His Land to Israel, the Jews. The scriptures, the prophecies are unequivocal, God has said it is theirs forever (Genesis 13:14-15).

ISBN: 978-1-909132-69-6, Pages: 136,
Format: Paperback, Published: 2018
Also available in eBook format!

Earnestly Contending for the State of Israel

The Jewish people are, and will continue to be God's people, He has not forgotten them or ever changed His mind where they are concerned. And now the time has come for the flag of Israel to be waved by the Jewish migrants who are gathering in their promised nation of Israel, today.

ISBN: 978-1-909132-71-9, Pages: 120,
Format: Paperback, Published: 2018
Also available in eBook format!

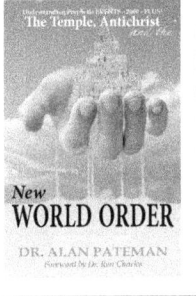

The Temple, Antichrist and the New World Order

The lives of everyone will be profoundly affected, even destroyed, culminating in the Battle of Armageddon. Many say that now is the time, it is this generation, that has been called to live out our destiny during the period that the ancients called the "birth pangs of the Messiah."

ISBN: 978-1-909132-73-3, Pages: 168,
Format: Paperback, Published: 2018
Also available in Hardback and eBook format!

The Antichrist, Rapture and the Battle of Armageddon

For the last four decades Russia has trained the military officers and intelligence staff of all of the nations listed in Ezekiel's prophecy. The phrase 'Prepare yourself' and 'be a guard for them' may indicate Russia's future role in providing arms and military leadership to the huge confederacy of nations.

ISBN: 978-1-909132-75-7, Pages: 128,
Format: Paperback, Published: 2017
Also available in eBook format!

All Books Available

at

APMI PUBLICATIONS

Email: publications@alanpatemanworldmissions.com
*Also Available from Amazon.com
and other retail outlets.*

*If you purchased this book through Amazon.com
or other and enjoyed reading it, or perhaps one of
my other books, I would be grateful if you could
take a couple of minutes to write a Customer
Review, many thanks.*

By Dr. Alan Pateman

The Reality of a Warrior

La Realta del Guerriero *(Italian Translation)*

Healing and Deliverance, A Present Reality

Control, A Powerful Force

His Life is in the Blood

Sexual Madness, In a Sexually Confused World *(co-authored with Jennifer Pateman)*

Apostles, Can the Church Survive Without Them?

Prayer, Ingredients for Successful Intercession, Part One

Prayer, Touching the Heart of God, Part Two

The Early Years, Anointed Generals Past and Present, Part One of Four

Revival Fires, Anointed Generals Past and Present, Part Two of Four

Why War, A Biblical Approach to the Armour of God and Spiritual Warfare

Forgiveness, the Key to Revival

His Faith, Positions us for Possession

Seduction & Control: Infiltrating Society and the Church

Kingdom Management for Anointed Prosperity

TONGUES, our Supernatural Prayer Language

Seven Pillars for Life and Kingdom Prosperity

WINNING by Mastering your Mind

Laying Foundations

Apostles and the Local Church

Preparations for Ministry

Developments and Provision

The Age of Apostolic Apostleship

Media, Spiritual Gateway *(co-authored with Jennifer Pateman)*

Israel, the Question of Ownership

Earnestly Contending for the State of Israel

The Temple, Antichrist and the New World Order

The Antichrist, Rapture and the Battle of Armageddon

Israel, the Church and the End Times

Introduction to all things APMI

Student's Handbook, Study Guide Volume 2

Empowered to Overcome

Equipped for Spiritual Warfare

Appropriations of African Territory

China, Covid-19, World Domination

Watchers of the 4 Kings

Coronavirus – Communist and Marxist Uprising

Changing Worlds, The Great Reset Deception

Davos and the Great Reset

The Ukraine Conflict – Waking Up to a New World Order

God's Anointed Well Diggers

Campus Set Up Helper, Study Guide Volume 3

Campus Guideline Handbook, Study Guide Volume 4

Instructor's Handbook, Study Guide Volume 5

The Fire of God that Gives us the Boldness to Break Free of Religion

Power or Influence

Breaking Out, Financial Freedom

God's Ways of Financial Increase

The Wonders of Christmas

Receiving Grace

Eagles of Destiny ...a Prophetic Concept

The Breakthrough is found in His Presence (31 Day Devotional)

Excellent Conduct

Kingdom Embrace

Believing in Kingdom Authority

By Your Consent

Living in His Overcoming Faith

The Culture of HONOUR

Truth for the Journey

I Need You, HOLY SPIRIT

The Apostolic Reformation and Restoration

The Nature of the Apostolic

The Triune God

The Road to Maturity

The Warrior's Garb

The Warrior's Stance

Three Faces of Control

Free to be Responsible

Fantasy Explosion for the Heavy Viewer

Breaking Free

From Bondage to Freedom

Jezebel Influencing the Church

New Age Seduction

Marriage Under Threat

The Controlling Syndrome

My Biography

The Python Spirit is Sent to Strangle our Success

The Power of Deliverance

Please, I Have a Question

Prophetic Trumpets and he that Overcomes

Kingdom Dimensions–Being Triumphant over all our Insecurities

Remind them of His Covenant Faithfulness (co-authored with Jennifer Pateman)

BY DR. JENNIFER PATEMAN

Sexual Madness, In a Sexually Confused World (co-authored with Alan Pateman)

Millennial Myopia, From a Biblical Perspective

Media, Spiritual Gateway (co-authored with Alan Pateman)

Truth Endures to All Generations

What comes first the Chicken or the Egg?

Writing Guidelines for Research Papers, Study Guide Volume 6

Writing Guidelines for Bachelor and Master Theses, Study Guide Volume 7

Writing Guidelines for Doctoral Dissertations, Study Guide Volume 8

Remind them of His Covenant Faithfulness (co-authored with Alan Pateman)

AVAILABLE FROM APMI PUBLICATIONS, AMAZON.COM AND OTHER RETAIL OUTLETS

www.ingramcontent.com/pod-product-compliance
Lightning Source LLC
Chambersburg PA
CBHW072009040426
42447CB00009B/1560